MARTIAL ARTS
TRAINING IN JAPAN

MARTIAL ARTS TRAINING IN JAPAN

A Guide for Westerners

David E. Jones

Tuttle Publishing
Boston · Rutland, Vermont · Tokyo

First published in 2001 by Tuttle Publishing, an imprint of Periplus Editions (HK) Ltd., with editorial offices at 153 Milk Street, Boston, MA 02109

Library of Congress Cataloging-in Publication Data
Jones, David E., 1942–
    Martial arts training in Japan: a guide for Westerners / by David E. Jones.
        p. cm.
    Includes bibliographical references.
    ISBN 0-8048-3270-6 (pbk.)
        1. Martial arts—Training—Japan. 2. Bushido. 3. Martial arts—Japan—Philosophy. I. Title.

GV1102.7.T7 J66 2001

Distributed by

North America, Latin America, Europe
Tuttle Publishing Distribution Center
Airport Industrial Park
364 Innovation Drive
North Clarendon, VT 05759-9436
Tel: (802) 773-8939
Toll free tel: (800) 526-2778
Fax: (802) 773-6993
Toll free fax: (800) 329-8885

Japan
Tuttle Publishing
RK Bldg. 2nd Floor
2-13-10 Shimo-Meguro
Meguro-Ku Tokyo 153 0064
Tel: (03) 5437 0171
Fax: (03) 5437 0755

Asian Pacific
Berkeley Books LTD
5 Little Road #08-01
Cemtex Industrial Bldg.
Singapore 536983
Tel: (65) 280 1330
Fax (65) 280 6290

05 04 03 02 01   9 8 7 6 5 4 3 2 1
Printed in the United States of America

Dedication

For all those teachers of the Warrior Way who
inspired me and encouraged me to stay the course.
(Gerald Brown Sensei, Thomas Cauley Shihan,
Mitsugi Saotome Shihan, Chan Poi Sifu, Dennis Hooker Shihan,
Asakuma Shihan, Ogata Shihan, Hanada Shihan)
Domo arigato gozaimasu!

 *Table of Contents*

Foreword

By Professor Thomas Cauley Kyoshi
Eighth-*dan* Chief Instructor, International Division, Sakugawa
Koshiki Shorinji-ryu karatedo and Yuishinkai kobujutsu

When I introduced Sakugawa Koshiki Shorinji-ryu karatedo to the United States in 1969, I found a willing following, but one that did not have the academic background or tenacity to understand the esoteric lessons of karatedo. In 1978, Professor David E. Jones entered my dojo in Orlando, Florida. I was at once impressed with his deep understanding of things Japanese and with his tireless pursuit of budo (the martial ways of Japan).

Since that time, David has continued to be an exemplary student, scholar, and proponent of Shorinji-ryu karatedo. He spent a year in Japan as a Fulbright scholar and taught in Fukuoka City. During this time he pursued several other martial Ways, including kyudo (*yabusame*) and Muso-ryu jyodo.

His book is a long overdue publication that will be of great use to martial arts teachers and students alike. The universality of budo, its worldwide practice and acceptance, a general deterioration of principles and precepts, and the desire of many to "return to the source," have all necessitated this book.

David's book is a valuable contribution to budo and directs attention to the very heart of the tenets and mores of the Japanese martial arts. I recommend it to every serious student and teacher of the Way.

Dr. Jones's attention to detail, exemplary knowledge of *komonjo* (ancient documents and archives), and his "warrior heart" make him the ideal author to guide the Western reader to the center of Japanese budo life and practice.

Preface

It is considered acceptable in Japan to ask martial arts teachers about their backgrounds (teachers, credentials, etc.). This is simply reasonable. As you would not put your life in the hands of an unqualified physician, you should not commit your time and money to study with a teacher who cannot demonstrate proof of certification. Martial arts teachers are generally interested, once an acceptable level of familiarity has been reached, in talking about their teachers and the often fascinating history of their ancient styles. Therefore, since this book purports to be a guide to martial arts training in Japan, I thought it would be appropriate that you know your guide's qualifications. The Japanese word for "teacher" is *sensei* and, means "born before" or "gone on before": in short, a guide.

I was awarded *shodan* (first-degree black belt rank) in aikido in 1973 by Saotome Mitsugi Shihan (master, exemplar), headmaster of the Aikido Schools of Ueshiba. In the spring of 1999 Saotome Shihan promoted me to the rank of *godan* (fifth-degree black belt). I was ranked to *nidan* (second-degree black belt) by Thomas Cauley Shihan, United States director of Sakugawa Koshiki Shorinji-ryu karatedo. In 1988–89, while teaching in Fukuoka, Japan on a Fulbright scholarship, I was promoted to *shodan* in Muso-ryu jodo, testing before Otofuji Shihan, then headmaster of the *ryu* (school, or style). At the Fukuoka Budokan I practiced kyudo (traditional Japanese archery) under Asakuma Hanshi (eighth-degree black belt) and was promoted to the rank of *shodan* after formal testing.

I have written a number of articles and presented numerous research papers at various anthropological conventions and meetings (the annual meeting of the American Anthropological Association, annual meeting of the Central States Anthropological Society, and the annual meeting of the Southwestern Anthropological Society) on various aspects of Japanese martial arts. My book *Women Warriors* (Brasseys, Inc.: McLean, Virginia, 1997) is a study of the worldwide female martial tradition. In addition, I was asked to contribute the foreword to Saotome Mitsugi Shihan's first book, *Aikido and The Harmony of Nature*. My tai chi ch'uan (Supreme Way of the Ultimate Fist) instructor, Chan Poi Sifu, grandmaster of Way Lum Praying Mantis kung fu, also asked me to write the foreword to his book, *The Fatal Flute Form*.

I have been teaching the martial arts aikido, Shorinji-ryu karatedo, and tai chi ch'uan for fifteen years. Presently I teach aikido two days a week at the University of Central Florida, where I am a professor of cultural anthropology, and two days a week at the Shin Dai Aikikai in Orlando, Florida, the largest aikido training facility in the area.

During my time in Japan I also trained in Komuso Zen (a Zen Buddhist sect whose name translates as "the followers of emptiness" or literally "emptiness, nothingness, priest") at Saikoji, a small temple on the grounds of Shofukuji in Fukuoka which is one of the most ancient Zen temples in Japan. The Komuso monks, easily identified by a helmet-like basketry hat (*tengai*) and the large bamboo flutes (*shakuhachi*) which they play as they wander on their alms-seeking rounds (*takuhatsu*), have a history that interestingly intertwines with that of the samurai, many of whom joined the Komuso and indelibly stamped it with their character.

My anthropological research has touched upon not only warfare and martial arts, but also religion, law, cross-cultural studies of education, and social control.

I have decided to write this guidebook in the first person, because if it is to be true to the essence and spirit of traditional martial arts practice in Japan, we have to come to know one another as best we can, even through the screen of the printed page. I will share my personal experiences of studying in Japan with you because, at least in broad outline, they will shortly become your experiences, too. Further, I will offer information of a practical nature regarding fees, finding a dojo, and practice schedules at various Japanese dojo, as well as cultural and historical materials pertaining to Japanese martial arts which one needs to be mindful of while training in a Japanese dojo.

The Japanese tale "Rashomon" provides classic insight into the various ways the same events are seen by different witnesses. I can only give you my reading on what I did and what I saw. My opinion sometimes differed from other Westerners. Some facets of budo training which I found to be boring, others found "Zenlike." What I considered to be the sadistic behavior of some *sempai* (senior students) others said was "hard training." Some of the experiences I found sublime—Zen, kyudo, jodo—others found "empty" and unproductive.

I have introduced myself to you by noting my various martial arts ranks—gifts from my generous teachers to this frail, awkward college professor—and though we cannot bow to each other in polite recognition, we have probably met and shared a moment of peace and harmony—sparring, perhaps. Maybe we were at the same seminar practicing basics under the critical eye of some noted sensei until we were ready to drop, dripping sweat, lungs heaving. Maybe we bumped elbows at the martial arts store looking over the latest books. Maybe we critically eyed each other in the *kata* competition at one of the local tournaments. I salute you and I envy you. *You are on your way to Japan!*

Acknowledgments

I wish to thank my wife, Jane M. Jones, for editorial assistance and support during the writing of this book; and Professor Thomas Cauley, United States Director of Sakugawa Koshiki Shorinji Ryu Karatedo, for his "Preface" and timely comments on the manuscript; and Dennis Hooker, Junko and Forrest Gillespie, Steve Fasen, and Wayne Van Horne for reading early drafts and offering their expert and timely comments. Finally, I wish to express deep gratitude to Mitsugi Saotome Shihan, Headmaster of the Aikido Schools of Ueshiba for consenting to be interviewed for this book. In the end, of course, final responsibility for the content of this work must, for better or for worse, rest with me.

MARTIAL ARTS
TRAINING IN JAPAN

Introduction

A very senior teacher of aikido, "the way of harmony," was once asked, "Sensei, what is the thing you like most about aikido?" His instant response was "The name."

The name for martial arts in Japan is *budo*, literally "military way," and often is loosely translated as "the way of the warrior." Taking a hint from the aikido sensei, we should pause to consider the meaning of the name of the art you are going to Japan to study.

Bu (war), the first Chinese ideogram or character, is a stylized image of a halberd-like Chinese weapon on the right and human efforts to repulse the weapons on the left. But literally *bu* means "to stop the attack" and suggests that the best way of stopping attacks is to live in peace, with the ability to defend that peace. The second character, *do*, depicts an image of a sailboat carrying its passenger to his or her final destination. It suggests a method of self-cultivation; a way or path, or a vehicle that takes you where you want to go. The teachers in any good Japanese martial arts school will expect you to practice budo, not some form of sport boxing or wrestling. Probably most of you who would seek to go to Japan for further martial arts study already know this; however, I mention it because I feel it is important to remind a student of the profound nature of martial arts practice as perceived by high-ranking Japanese teachers.

But which is the budo for you? Once I overheard a new student ask my tai chi ch'uan teacher, Chan Poi Sifu, which martial art was the best one. Teacher Chan replied, "Right hand, right foot. Left hand, left foot. Block. Punch. Kick. All the same." Then, pointing to his head and his heart, he concluded, "The only difference is here."

It is also true that all roads lead to Rome, they just start at different points. Some people feel comfortable with an art in which they can wrestle with one another or spar on a regular basis and they start there. Others would find an art with an emphasis on competitive fighting to be distracting, even immature. Some aspiring students are attracted to the arts of the famous Japanese sword, while others wish to study *kobudo* and learn to manipulate the ancient farm-implement weaponry of Okinawa—the *nunchaku* (rice flail), *tonfa* (rice-grinding-wheel handle), *kama* (sickle), *bo* (long staff), *sai* (three-pronged wheel pin), and *jutte* (policeman's baton). Other less well-known kobudo weaponry include the use of sea-turtle shell as a shield and spear-head as a bladed weapon, and the martial use of the boat oar, or *ro*.

The point is to pick a road and begin the journey. Rome will be at the end of it somewhere, but that's not the important point. The nature of the journey—the Way—is the primary concern.

The most popular Japanese martial arts in terms of numbers of students are *karatedo* ("the way of the empty hand"), *judo* ("the gentle way"), *kendo* ("the way of the sword"), and *aikido* ("the way of harmony"). These four warrior ways are also the most widespread and visible around the world. Most who travel to Japan to study martial arts will probably practice one of the four major arts. That being the case, I will offer a brief history of each art, a description of its physical appearance and practice goals, my observations concerning who would most and least benefit from the practice of that art, and instructions on how to find a suitable dojo that will serve your interests. I will also include information on training in *iaido* ("the way of drawing the sword"), *jodo* ("the way of the staff"), and *naginatado* ("the way of the halberd"): three archaic weapons arts that are widespread in Japan, but relatively little known outside that country. Finally, I will discuss training in *ninjutsu* ("the art of stealth").

Another important question to ask yourself is "What is my purpose for going to Japan to train in the martial arts?" What do you want from your experience in a Japanese training environment? Personal challenge, knowledge, a good workout, meditation, aerobics, self-defense training, traditional art experience, self-confidence, a chance to experience a living history? Any traditional martial arts dojo will touch on all of the above topics over time. At the same time one can find teachers, martial arts styles, and schools that naturally— or because of commercial considerations—cater to a particular martial arts training approach. There are many: the physical intensity of judo; the meditative effects of iaido; the flow of aikido; the surge and snap of karatedo, the auditory and physical clamor of kendo; the stateliness of kyudo (traditional archery); the esoteric mysteries of ninjutsu.

Studying a completely different art from the one you train in at home might also be worth considering. It is an ancient dictum that creativity is stimulated by contrast. You might consider practicing more than one art. You are probably not going to be training in Japan long enough to fundamentally affect your mind/body, but you could take the opportunity to more broadly educate yourself. Most advanced martial arts teachers are, in fact, ranked in more than one art. To really know what you are doing necessitates knowing what you are not doing . . . and why. *Bonsai* (the culturing of miniature trees), *ikebana* (flower arranging), *sado* (the tea ceremony), and *go* (Japanese chess) are also excellent ways to polish the warrior soul.

Don't dismiss these arts as being unfitting to the training of a *budoka*, a student/practitioner of the warrior way. The mental tension created in the warfare of the *go* board can be exhausting. For me, the practice of the tea ceremony was the most mentally and physically draining art I practiced while in Japan. The very precise *kata* (pre-arranged form) of the tea ceremony, its slow and measured pace, the ritual requirements of guest and host, both at the physical and verbal level, would leave me exhausted. This reveals more about me during the time I was in Japan than the tea ceremony itself. I would have preferred practicing karatedo *kihon waza* (basic technique) in full *kiai* mode than spending the same two hours under the intense scrutiny of the tea sensei. The power and elegance of karatedo gave me energy, while the precision and dignity of tea took it from me.

That experience taught me something about myself as a budoka. When I could disengage my logical mind from the acts of my body, the training would produce energy as a by-product of practice. Practicing basic karatedo techniques leaves one no time or energy to think. But with the tea ceremony, I was trying to make my body act with the precision required while my mind was full of "Remember to do this and not that " and "Let's see, do I rotate the bowl three times or two times before sipping," and "I hope I'm not making too much of a fool of myself." Another way to put it is that until you can see the relatedness between the tea ceremony or a game of *go* and the martial art you practice, you are not practicing your martial art at a very high level.

The lesson here is universal and sounds almost mystical, but really is not. The mind has to cease discursiveness for the body to learn. When the two are vying for position, the result is that you are working against yourself, with the effect of simply exhausting your energy. You are working for perfection of an act that when done correctly you will never witness, such as a judo throw, the shot of an arrow, a correctly timed combination in *kumite* (sparring; literally: "exchange of hands"). Experienced martial arts sensei will tell you that they often experience spontaneous techniques which seem to occur when the discursive mind is not paying attention.

Occasionally, when teaching aikido, I will invite my demonstration partner to attack freely. Sometimes my response is conditioned by decades of aikido practice and is usually a basic technique—and sometimes the defensive technique I use seems to come out of nowhere! I see the attack come, and the next thing I see is the attacker on the dojo floor. If the technique felt right—a condition I cannot define—I clap my hands and invite the students to practice the technique. As they begin, I study my senior students to find out what I just did, because in a very true way "I" was not there when it happened. If you hang around to congratulate yourself on how good you look in *kata*, you will progress much less than if you rid yourself of the ego observer.

Even as I write this, it sounds like so much mystical drivel, but it is not! It is the natural outcome of sound practice over time.

My aikido sensei described the experience of spontaneous technique as being possessed by the spirit of his deceased teacher. I remember thinking, "Interesting, the sensei believes in spirit possession." Many years later, when I experienced this sensation personally, I understood what he was talking about. However, I did not see it as literally being possessed by a spirit, for my cultural and educational background made that assumption too much of a reach. It did occur to me that aikido was literally shaped by the experience of its founder, Ueshiba Morihei Shihan, and an experience of spontaneous technique was, in a manner of speaking, an act of being possessed by the master's art. Where else did the spontaneous technique come from? My body and mind had been molded over many years by continuous training in the basic techniques of Ueshiba Shihan's art and when it found expression in my creative acts as an aikido teacher it was as if Ueshiba Shihan, who had become one with his art, was present in me through his art. My aikido sensei called this type of experience "the miracle of hard training."

Karatedo: The Way of the Empty Hand

Karatedo has a wonderful story of origin. The orthodox account is that karatedo originated in India. The martial arts of contemporary India at this point in their evolution, however, look much more like kung fu, with its complex "animal forms" and great variety of exotic weaponry, than the austere art of modern karatedo. Kung fu does not, in fact, point to a particular type of Chinese martial art but, as the literal translation of kung fu ("effort") suggests, to any skill derived over time through hard training. It may be said that kung fu is at least partially derived from India and that later karatedo evolved from an ancient branch of kung fu.

The ancient story tells of Bodhidharma (Japanese: Daruma; Chinese: Tamo), the twenty-eighth patriarch of Buddhism, and his arrival in China in the sixth century A.D. on a mission to revitalize Chinese Buddhism. In the company of his Sherpa guides (traditionally described as eighteen in number), Bodhidharma briefly visited with Emperor Wu and then moved into residence at the monastery of Shaolin-szu (Japanese: Shorinji), "Temple of the Young Pine Trees." (Some versions of the story claim that he founded the famous Shaolin temple.) Finding the resident monks too weak to follow his rigorous monastic regimen, he taught them a style of martial art which he derived from the Kshatriya (warrior) caste of India, combining an emphasis on strong diaphragm breathing, characteristic of Indian yoga, with an evolving admixture of the local *kempo,* or Chinese methods of unarmed combat.

The connection between Buddhism and warrior arts seems contradictory at first glance. However, it should be remembered that Siddhartha Gautama, the Buddha, was a member of the warrior caste of India and, in fact, won his royal bride in an archery contest.

Over time, the Shaolin martial arts adapted to local conditions and it is suggested in the common explanation that karatedo developed in the south of China, where the short, stocky agricultural workers with their strongly developed arms and upper bodies developed the Shaolin art in a direction that would come to be recognized as contemporary karatedo.

The story then moves to Okinawa, the main island of the Ryukus, the chain of islands that stretches south from Japan to Taiwan. Okinawa had long been a point of contact between Chinese and Japanese cultures. It was here that the *te,* or strong hand techniques (striking, punching) which had evolved as a regional style in Okinawa over centuries, began to mix and blend with the *kempo* of China with its more rounded and flowing techniques. The evolving combination was called "T'ang Hand" after the great Chinese dynasty that had such an impact on the development of Japanese culture. The Chinese characters for "T'ang Hand" were later read as "Empty (*kara*) Hand (*te*)."

The early *karatedoka* of Okinawa developed, in addition, the art of kobudo as they came into continual hostile contact with Japanese samurai clans (particularly the Satsuma clan of southern Kyushu) who raided Okinawa for countless generations. To this day, one sees kobudo weapons, such as the *nunchaku, sai, tonfa,* and *kama,* in traditional karate dojo.

In 1917 Funakoshi Gichin, a renowned Okinawan educator, was invited by the Japanese Ministry of Education to give public demonstrations of karatedo in the main islands of Japan. His first trip was so successful that he returned in 1923 to take up permanent residence. In 1936 he inaugurated the first karate dojo in the main islands of Japan. It was called Shotokan, or "Shoto's House." The name came from Funakoshi Sensei's pen name, "Shoto," which means "wind through the pine trees." Today, Shotokan karatedo continues as one of the major karatedo styles.

Influenced by Professor Funakoshi, martial arts practitioners established dojo for various karatedo styles. Okinawan Miyagi Chojun founded the Goju style. Yamaguchi Gogen, a Japanese student of Master Miyagi, created his own version of the Goju style. Otsuka Hironori combined jujutsu with the "T'ang Hand" and arrived at his Wado style. Around this time the "T'ang Hand" reading was dropped and the "Empty Hand" adopted, perhaps because of growing Japanese nationalistic sentiments against China. Although some of the old masters of Okinawa resented the name change, it fit not only the nationalism of the times but also the Zen thrust of karatedo. Master Funakoshi explained it as follows (Williams, 1975:132):

> As a mirror's polished surface reflects whatever stands before it and
> a quiet valley carries even small sounds, so must the student of
> karate render his mind empty of selfishness and wickedness in an
> effort to react appropriately to anything he might encounter. This
> is the meaning of kara or "empty" in karate.

Japanese karatedo has come to incorporate philosophies important to the Japanese. Whereas modern Japanese karatedoka may philosophize about Zen, and "no mind," and *satori* (enlightenment), the Okinawan stylist, for the most part, was simply trying to hit and kick as hard as possible and incorporated philosophical underpinnings such as *ki* (intrinsic energy) and *hara* (the emotional, spiritual and physical center of the body) to assist in that primary objective.

The later history of Japanese karatedo is well documented because it is relatively modern; however, the orthodox origin tale involving Bodhidharma, the Shaolin temple, and the Sherpa guides may be "wild history," as one of my Japanese teachers called it. I was first introduced to this concept while being taught the oral tradition of the origin of the Komuso Zen sect.

One afternoon, Hanada Shihan sat me down in the *zendo* (meditation hall) of Saikoji and told me the story of the founder of Komuso Zen, a wild Chinese monk named P'u-hua (known as Fuke in

Japanese). Fuke was a compatriot of the great Chinese master Lin-chi (Japanese: Rinzai), the inspirational source of the Rinzai sect of Zen Buddhism that developed in Japan during the Kamakura period.

After setting the stage, Hanada Shihan, obviously enjoying himself, told the story of Fuke. Rinzai loved Fuke although Fuke was considered by his fellow monks to be crazy. He slept in the fields or in the barns, rarely washed, took no disciples, and was constantly interrupting Rinzai at his important work as head of a large T'ang-dynasty Buddhist monastery. For example, one day Rinzai had invited some of the local dignitaries to the monastery for a pleasant meal. As the mayor and his staff enjoyed the fine food and stimulating conversation of Rinzai, Fuke showed up uninvited. He turned over Rinzai's table and addressed the dignitaries with, "Ho-yang is a new bride. Mu-t'a is a Ch'an granny, and Rinzai is a young menial, but he has the eye." He then left the room. The irate guests raged against the lout Fuke, but Rinzai only said, "There goes a truly enlightened being."

Young monks, on hearing that Rinzai had announced Fuke to be an enlightened man, sought out Fuke for his mentorship. Fuke, true to form, simply rang his bell in their faces every time they asked him a religious question and recited,

> *Coming as brightness, I strike the brightness;*
> *Coming as darkness, I strike the darkness;*
> *Coming from the four quarters and eight directions,*
>   *I hit like a whirlwind;*
> *Coming from the empty sky, I lash like a flail.*

When the monks returned to Rinzai and told him what nonsense Fuke was uttering, Rinzai simply said, "He is truly an enlightened man."

Fuke's behavior in the days leading up to his death was characteristic of the man. Hanada Shihan said that one day Fuke, dragging a coffin, announced to the people who had gathered to watch him ring his bell and preach his crazy sermon, "Tomorrow Fuke will cross over at the North Gate. Be there." He was announcing the precise time of his passing, a behavior periodically recorded for spiritual leaders of the time.

On the following day all gathered at the North Gate, but when Fuke arrived he looked about him and said, "No. Today is not good. Tomorrow, Fuke will cross over at the South Gate. Be there."

The next day, the crowd assembled at the South Gate, but when Fuke arrived he said, "No. Today is not the right day. Tomorrow, Fuke will cross over at the West Gate. Be there."

On the third day the crowd of onlookers was greatly reduced. When Fuke dragged his coffin up he looked at the people standing in the road, looked at the sky, and then said, "No. Today is not exactly right. Tomorrow, Fuke will cross over at the East Gate. Be there."

On the following day no one appeared to witness Fuke's passing. He looked around him, stared at the sky, and said, "Today is the perfect day to cross over." He placed his coffin outside the East Gate and sat on it. When a farmer passed on his way to market Fuke said, "Sir, would you please nail me into my coffin and then go tell Master Rinzai that Fuke has crossed over."

The farmer did as Fuke asked. Rinzai, on hearing the news, rushed with his retinue to the East Gate, but upon opening Fuke's coffin they found it empty except for one sandal. As they stared into the open coffin the faint ringing of Fuke's bell was heard in the sky. Today, one of the major pieces in the *shakuhachi* repertoire of the Komuso Zen sect is called "A Bell Ringing in the Empty Sky."

As Hanada Shihan told the story I took notes as fast as I could. Finally, he paused and said, "Jones Sensei, as an educated man you should know that this is…," he searched for an English word, "…wild history." Using one of my most often-used Japanese expressions I said to him, "I don't understand, Sensei."

Hanada Shihan explained that perhaps because temple records were so routinely lost to fire over the centuries and subsequently rewritten, their historical value, as Westerners understand history, is confused. The stories are not intended as literal history in the Western sense of scientific history, but as an emotional or spiritual context, a rich and satisfying explanation of serious and auspicious origins. Did Fuke say what Hanada Shihan suggested? Who knows? Hanada Shihan doesn't. That is not the point anyway. It is the spirit of the story that is important. The story says that the Komuso sect was derived from a unique, fearless and humorous man whom the great Rinzai characterized as an enlightened being.

Returning to the oral traditional of karatedo, we might ask if Bodhidharma was a real man. Did he actually initiate martial arts training at Shaolin temple? Was he instrumental in the founding of Zen Buddhism? Was he a major influence on Hui Neng, the sixth patriarch of Zen Buddhism in China? Who knows! Hui Neng's name, by the way, does not even appear on lists of early Zen masters in China and no proof exists that someone named Bodhidharma arrived in central China at the time the legend states. (These observations are from a Chinese scholar from Columbia University who was in Japan translating antique Chinese Zen texts and comparing them to Japanese texts). But, as Hanada Shihan suggests, these are not the important points to stress when considering the origin of karatedo. Read the Bodhidharma tale this way: karatedo was created from an ancient system of mind/body/spirit coordination that has taken its specific form from the cultures in which it has traveled, being influenced along the way by Indian yoga, Chinese Taoism, Ch'an Buddhism, and *kempo*; and Okinawan and Japanese martial arts, philosophy, and culture. Linear history is an impossible ideal. Buddha suggested that to attempt to trace history was like following the tracks of a bird as it flew across the sky. Hanada Shihan noted that the value of an origin tale is found in how it affects the behavior of those who accept it, and not in scholarly questions as to its reality.

It is important for Westerners to understand that human behavior is conditioned in an overwhelming fashion by culture. If we try to apply our culture's notion of linear scientific history to the "histories" of the Japanese martial arts, we will be making an error. Western history objectively identifies sequences of events: "A" before "B," "B" before "C," etc. Japanese oral tradition on the other hand creates a temporal context, an atmosphere, a program of tales and heroes that coherently explains the "feeling" or "spirit" of the art as opposed to the Western desire to know that a particular art's history is "right" from a Western perspective. "Right" is largely determined by cultural constraints.

One late afternoon after I had been in Japan about a month, I was walking across the campus of Seinan Gakuin, one of the colleges at which I taught, when I heard a familiar sound coming from the rear of a classroom building. *"Ichi! Ni! San!"* (one, two, three) a man's voice barked. On *"San!"* a great shout *(kiai)*, arose from the hidden body of students. There were a number of possibilities, but I guessed that it was a karatedo group practicing a combination of blocks, punches, and kicks with a *kiai* marking the final technique in the series. I was right.

I took a seat on a bench about fifty feet from the *karatedoka*, and as the shadows deepened around the ancient pine trees that dotted the campus, I watched the *karatedoka* drilling back and forth to the commands: *Ichi!* (front snap kick), *Ni!* (rising block), *San!* (reverse punch), the *kiai* sounding with the reverse punch. It was very familiar, and though I was on the other side of the world from the place of my birth, I felt at home as I watched the Japanese *karatedoka* in their drills. To the outsider, karatedo looks like a method of fighting, full of kicking, punching, and violent shouts, but in truth it is a physical embodiment of a message of peace and the heroic acceptance of our common destiny.

The sound of strong, focused breathing. The snap of the *dogi* (practice uniform) sleeve when a student's reverse punch worked well. The random music of the senior students as they sparred at the end of class, joking lightly with one another. I found myself watching a young Japanese white belt struggling with basic techniques and in my mind I coached him as I would a student of mine back in the States: "Relax your shoulders. Bend your knees. Don't wobble." Karatedo has a hard and noble beauty that will come to you after years of relaxing your shoulders, bending your knees, and steadying your posture. In my travels around Japan I saw many karatedo groups, each with its slightly differing ways of performing similar techniques but all giving me the feeling of deep familiarity. The strong common thread of karatedo is present no matter which of the many styles (public and "hidden") is practiced, and there are hundreds of such styles.

I remember a karatedo class practicing one evening on a beach at Satsuma. From my vantage point about fifty yards away in a formal garden on a hill overlooking the bay, the white *dogi* of the students glowed as they moved over the black volcanic sand beach. The class began a torturous exercise in which the students kicked as high as

13

they could, as slowly as they could. The sensei spaced the students randomly on the beach with each apparently on his own. The sun began to disappear into the sea and the *dogi* of the karatedo students took on a misty gray hue as they balanced unmoving in a kicking posture. It looked like some giant had been practicing calligraphy using pearl ink on black paper.

The basic plan of most karatedo classes might entail twenty to twenty-five minutes of warm-up exercises and maybe some strength drills. This will usually be followed by *kihon waza*, generally practiced as students move up and down the dojo floor, performing the required techniques to the guttural cadence of the sensei or a senior student. *Kihon waza* may be followed by one- or two-step sparring in which the basic techniques are taught in combinations and practiced with a partner, one acting the attacker for the other. Next may come work on *kata*, the choreographed series of techniques basic to the style being practiced. In an hour-and-a-half class all of the above may be encountered plus, on occasion, weapons practice (usually *bo, sai, tonfa, nunchaku, kama*) or a lecture on some important point of history or philosophy by the sensei. A good karatedo sensei will have many surprises to ensure that the training does not become stale. One night you may find mixed into the meat of the class a mini-seminar on binding attackers with short lengths of rope, or the use of the headband (*hatchimaki*) as a self-defense tool, or specific customs related to sword handling. Sometimes you might find the entire class devoted to sparring or methods of meditation or breathing exercises. There is always a formal beginning and ending to karatedo classes marked by order and expressions of gratitude. The sensei, of course, can change the plan of a class at any time. Time and space belong to the sensei while in the dojo.

The three main themes in one's study of karatedo are *kihon waza* (basic techniques), *kata* (prescribed practice forms), and *kumite* (sparring, or literally, "exchange of hands"). The quality of anything one does in karatedo is grounded in basic techniques; a truism for all aspects of life, of course. The basic techniques of karatedo are much more than collections of a style's fundamental physical techniques. Each technique offers an experience of our common fate: birth, death, remanifestation. Each technique is the first and last thing you do for the rest of your life. Each basic technique is a world in itself, having its own feeling, its own meaning, its own spirit. There is always hope. We are born. We pass away. We live again.

Kata leads one to focus on the life vehicles we use to get us where we are going. The first *kata* series in Japanese karatedo is called Heian, "peace." *Kata* is about shoulders that carry burdens. It is about going and returning, and being stronger on your return. It carries a similar purport to one of the major scriptures of Zen Buddhism, the *Prajna Paramita Sutra*, which talks of going and returning. The character for "Way" (Japanese: *do*) is based on an image of a sailboat, a vehicle that carries one "over" and then returns. Another interpretation of the character for *do* is that it represents a man standing at a crossroads preparing to make a major life decision (artist and calligrapher Zhou Quangwi favors the later interpretation).

Finally, *kumite* is the battlefield where basic techniques as well as the myriad transitions from one technique to another learned in *kata* training come together in the spontaneous act of sparring, or *kumite*. Karate dojo can differ quite a lot on the degree to which they emphasize *kumite* over *kata*. In some dojo, *kumite* is a minor component of training, and *kata* is given great weight. In others, the situation is reversed. The common thread will be *kihon waza*. This is the heart of any budo.

Look at *kata*, *kihon waza*, and *kumite* as you would look at a tree. We see it because of light, but we don't know what we see without the dark that sets off the light. Try looking at the shadows of a tree and not the lighted parts. I think that in karatedo *kata* is something like that. In *kata* I see students hurrying from one light point to the next, but the string that holds it all together, the transitional movements, is reacted to almost as a nuisance. A mature student understands that the light's brightness is directly related to the quality of the surrounding darkness. A technique in any art is only as good as the support brought to bear in the actualizing of the technique's goal. You must set your hips correctly before your punch or kick has any meaning. It is the spaces that make solid things useful, as the *Tao Te Ching* shows us. What is a window without an opening? It is what is not there in a cup that makes it useful. Can a doorway be solid? The name *karate* means the hand is empty in the way that the universe is empty, i.e. full of promise and possibilities.

Karatedo is one of the most widely adaptable of the Japanese martial arts. Children can train in karatedo tailored for them and gain great benefit. Elderly people would find interesting exercise in a karatedo designed for them. The possibilities of karatedo are great. Just make sure you find a karatedo group that is teaching what you want to learn in the way you wish to learn it.

Although, as noted, the basic techniques are all fundamentally the same, some stark contrasts exist in attitude and level of intensity in the practice of karatedo. This is true with all closely allied arts. In Chinese t'ai chi ch'uan, for example, though there are a number of family styles (Chen, Li, Yang, Wu), only thirteen basic postures are used. Likewise, all karatedo styles will have punches, strikes, blocks, parries, leg sweeps, snap kicks, round-house kicks, thrusting kicks, jumping kicks, joint techniques, etc.

Another common theme in many karatedo classes is the spirited chanting of *dojokun* (precepts of the dojo), at the end of class, with each *ryu* having its own variation. Sometimes, *dojokun* are simply posted and are meant to be contemplated by the serious karatedo student. Here are Funakoshi Gichin's *Nijukun* ("Twenty Precepts"):

1. Karate is not only dojo training.
2. Don't forget that karate begins with a bow and ends with a bow.
3. In karate, never attack first.
4. One who practices karate must follow the way of justice.
5. First you must know yourself. Then you can know others.
6. Spiritual development is paramount; technical skills are merely means to the end.
7. You must release your mind.
8. Misfortune comes out of laziness.
9. Karate is lifelong training.
10. Put karate into everything you do.
11. Karate is like hot water. If you do not give heat constantly it will again become cold.
12. Do not think you have to win. Think that you do not have to lose.

13. Victory depends on your ability to tell vulnerable points from invulnerable ones.
14. Move according to your opponent.
15. Consider your opponent's hands and legs as you would sharp swords.
16. When you leave home, think that millions of opponents are waiting for you.
17. Ready position for beginners and natural position for advanced students.
18. Kata is one thing. Engaging in a real fight is another.
19. Do not forget (a) strength and weakness of power; (b) expansion and contraction of the body; (c) slowness and speed of techniques.
20. Devise at all times [i.e., be creative].

A more typical and "chantable" *dojokun* could be rendered in English as:

Attention! Seek Perfection of Character!
Attention! Be Faithful!
Attention! Endeavor!
Attention! Respect Others!
Attention! Refrain from Violent Behavior!

Since Okinawa is considered a cradle of karatedo development, a few of the major styles of Okinawan karatedo will be considered first. The umbrella organization, the Zen Okinawa Karatedo Renmei (All Okinawa Karatedo Federation), has a long and complex history. In April of 1918, Funakoshi Gichin, Oshiro Chodo, Hanashiro Chomo, Chibana Choshin, Mabuni Kenwa, Tokuda Anbun, Gusukuma Shimpan, Tokumura Masumi, and Ishigawa Ryugyo formed the Karate Kenkyu Kai (Karate Preservation Association). Also, in 1924, Miyagi Chojun, Kyoda Juhatsu, Shinzato Jinan, Shiroma Koki, Kyan Chotoku and Motobu Choki met in Naha city to form the Karate Kenkyu Association. In March 1926 the two organizations merged to form the Okinawa Karate Club.

By 1956 representatives of the four major Okinawan Karatedo styles—Uechi-ryu, Goju-ryu, Shorin-ryu, and Matsubayashi-ryu—

met in Naha and formed the Okinawa Karatedo Renmei (Okinawa Karatedo Federation). Finally, in February of 1967, the various organizations devoted to the study and preservation of Okinawan karatedo reorganized to form the Zen Okinawa Karatedo Renmei. This organization recognized Goju-ryu, Shorin-ryu, Matsubayashi-ryu, Shobayashi-ryu, Tozan-ryu, Shorinji-ryu, and Chuba Shorin-ryu. The volatility of these organizations is apparent in their histories. In 1973 Goju-ryu left the organization; in 1974, Tozan-ryu left. Then on November 30, 1975, the Ryukyu Kobudo Hozon Shinkokai joined the All Okinawa Karatedo Federation. In 1981 another rift among Okinawan practitioners occurred. One group, the Yamato-ha, joined the Zen Nihon Karatedo Renmei (part of the Japan Athletics Association), whereas the Okinawa-ha, strongly loyal to their native Okinawa, refrained from joining another karatedo association merely for the sake of being recognized by Japanese institutions.

The complex fission and fusion of karatedo groups is somehow inherent in their natures, the dynamics of which would make for a good academic study. The psycho-political turmoil caused by these political rifts can be very disorienting for students. Keep in mind, however, that although past history may be mildly interesting, living fully in the present is the point of it all. Let the political people play their games. Your job is to practice as hard as you can. Who is or is not chairman of such-and-such a karatedo organization obviously has nothing to do with the necessity of your developing good posture, strength, stance, center, breath, stamina, movement, structure, and speed, and rendering these fundamental physical virtues through the techniques of your chosen style.

To provide specific direction to finding and practicing an Okinawan style of karatedo, I will focus on Okinawan Shorin-ryu ("Young Forest Style") and Okinawan Goju-ryu ("Hard and Soft Way"). Once you have found your way into the social context of Goju-ryu or Shorin-ryu, directions to contact other Okinawan styles, such as Chito-ryu, will be accessible. Okinawa is not that big an island.

Shorin-ryu

In 1960 the Okinawan Karate Federation promoted Nakazato Shugoro to eighth-degree black belt and *kyoshi* (a "spiritual" rank).

Nakazato Sensei was born in Naha City on August 14, 1919. His karatedo training began in 1935 under Ishu Seiichi. In 1946 he began a long history of instruction under the famous master of karatedo Chibana Choshin Shihan. In 1951 Nakazato Sensei helped Chibana Sensei to open his Dai Ichi Dojo in Naha City. Three years later, Nakazato Sensei received his *shihan menkyojo* and became Master Chibana's *shihan dai* (personal assistant). Nakazato's work with Chibana Sensei was so effective that he was commissioned by Chibana Sensei to found the Shorin-ryu Shorinkan Nakazato Dojo in Naha City at Aza. When Master Chibana passed away, Nakazato Shugoro inherited the leadership of Okinawan Shorin-ryu karatedo.

The office of Nakazato Shugoro, president and grandmaster of Shorin-ryu, is located at 264 Aja, Naha-shi, Okinawa-ken 900-0003, Japan. The North American Headquarters may be reached by contacting Frank Hargrove Sensei (eighth-degree black belt) at 2034 Nickerson Blvd., Hampton, Virginia, or by calling (757) 850-8500. Mr. Hargrove's e-mail address is karate@usa.net.

Goju-ryu

This popular style of karatedo was founded in the 1920s by Master Miyagi Chojun of Naha City. The style combines Okinawan (hard) and Shaolin kung fu (soft) techniques. Several Chinese systems, in fact, were studied by Master Miyagi and incorporated into the pure Okinawan styles (te), notably White Crane Kung Fu, Pakua Chang, I Ch'uan, and t'ai chi ch'uan. Goju-ryu is a close-range fighting style emphasizing kicking to lower-body targets, joint manipulations, and dynamic breath training along with the typical Okinawan karatedo techniques of blocking, striking, kicking, punching, and parrying.

Miyagi Chojun chose the name Goju-ryu from the third precept listed in the Goju-ryu text called "Eight Poems of the Fists":

1. The mind is one with heaven and earth.
2. The circulatory rhythm of the body is similar to the cycle of the sun and the moon.
3. The way of inhaling and exhaling is hardness and softness.
4. Act in accordance with time and change.

5. Techniques will occur in the absence of conscious thought.

6. The feet must advance and retreat, separate and meet.

7. The eyes do not miss even the slightest change.

8. The ears listen well in all directions.

The following are some of the Goju-ryu karate dojo to be found in Okinawa. Contact with any one of these clubs will put you in contact with many others of the same style.

Mr. Iha Koshin Jundokan Hombu Dojo
2-6-13 Asato, Naha-shi, Okinawa-ken 902-0067, Japan
Tel: (098) 863-0011

Mr. Yamashiro Katsuya
Higaonna Dojo
42-22-3 Chome Makishi , Naha-shi, Okinawa-ken 900-0013, Japan

Mr. Ikemiyagi Masaaki
Meibukan Goju-ryu Okinawa Dojo
3-29-17 Minami Tobaru, Okinawa-shi, Okinawa-ken 904-0035, Japan

Mr. Hokama Yasuaki
Meibukan Goju-ryu Ueda Dojo
535-1 Ueda, Tomishiro-son, Okinawa-ken 901-0243, Japan

Mr. Hokama Tetsuhiro
Okinawa Goju-ryu Kenshikai Karate / Kobudo So Hombu
277-33 Yonashiro, Nishihara-cho, Okinawa-ken 903-0111, Japan

Mr. Uechi Tsutomu
Goju-ryu Kokusai Karatedo Renmei
90 Nishizato, Hirara-shi, Okinawa-ken 906-0012, Japan

Mr. Miyazato Eiko
Gokenkan Dojo
442 Asato, Naha-shi, Okinawa-ken 902-0067, Japan
e-mail: GOKENKAN@aol.com

Chito-ryu

This ryu (like all others, no doubt) demonstrates the fission and fusion of different styles that characterize the history of the majority of Japanese martial arts, ancient and modern. An Okinawan karatedo master, Dr. Chitose Tsuyoshi (1898–1984), created Chito-ryu by combining the elements he liked from Okinawan Shorei-ryu and Shorin-ryu karatedo. His goal was to rationally consider the medical implications of traditional karatedo practice and to find a system which would have maximum martial and health effects and minimal detrimental elements, such as long-term injury from the practice of certain joint techniques, chronic lower back pain from incorrect stance and movement instruction, and tendonitis in the elbow from snapping the elbow while punching. Chito-ryu, like all traditionally based forms of karatedo, focuses on the three main pillars of karate practice: kihon waza (basic techniques), kata (form), and kumite (sparring). Chitose Shihan called his style Chito-ryu karatedo to honor the Chinese roots of Okinawan karate: chi is a character meaning one thousand years old; to is the character for T'ang China.

The following is a list of Chito-ryu Karate Federation dojo and their locations:

Chikuenjuku (Fukuoka)
Daidokan (Tochigi)
Edogawa, Koto, Adachi (Tokyo)
Fukuyama (Hiroshima)
Genryukan (Miyazaki)
Kenshinkan (Osaka)
Kenshinkan (Shizuoka)
Metaabaru (Saga)
Nisshokan (Okayama)
Omiya (Saitama)

For more detailed information, write to:

International Chito-ryu Karatedo Association
c/o Miyazaki Naomi
Shinjokan
4332 Nozu Ryuhoku , Kumamoto-shi
Kumamoto-ken 869-4805, Japan
Tel: (96) 552-2251

Shotokan

In 1949 the JKA (Japan Karate Association) was formed with Master Funakoshi Gichin as head instructor. The style he taught was referred to as Shotokan karatedo. In 1957 the Japanese government recognized the JKA as the only legal nonprofit karatedo organization in Japan. Answerable to the Japanese Ministry of Education (Mombusho) Shotokan is probably the most widely proliferated karatedo style, with several thousand qualified instructors worldwide.

When Master Funakoshi passed away a split occurred in the ranks of his followers, a very common occurrence in karatedo history, as I have noted. The modern JKA is strictly the public face of the Shotokan style of Master Nakayama Masatoshi (now deceased). Karatedo sensei Nishiyama, Oshima, Ueki, and Kanezawa also joined Nakayama. The original Funakoshi school was called Shotokai, and those who chose to maintain it included Funakoshi Gigo and Aoki Hiroyuki. One of my budo teachers has commented, "Today, Shotokai is the original following of Funakoshi, and Shotokan follows the neo-budo path."

The reason for the split between the Shotokan and the Shotokai lies most obviously in the reactions to a point of etiquette concerning who should organize the funeral ceremony for Master Funakoshi, who had passed away on April 26, 1957. Clearly there were hidden agendas behind this extraordinary and rancorous situation, issues that led to the political struggle concerning the funeral. But do you have to take a position? Of course not! The visiting karatedo student should always stay out of local politics. Your job is to work in the dojo until you have no more energy for politics and related forms of mischief.

Questions concerning training in Shotokan karatedo in Japan may be answered by contacting the Japan Karate Association or Shotokan International:

Japan Karate Association Headquarters
6-2 Ebisu Nishi 1-chome, Shibuya-ku, Tokyo 150, Japan
Tel: (03) 3476-4611 / (03) 3476-1431
Fax: (03) 3476-0322

Shotokan Karatedo International General Headquarters
2-1-20 Minami Kugahara, Ota-ku, Tokyo 146, Japan
Tel: (03) 3754-5481
Fax: (03) 3754-5483
Website: http://plaza27.mbn.or.jp/~kkaname/skif/skif_e.htm

Japan Karatedo Federation Gojukai

As noted earlier, an offshoot of the Okinawan Goju-ryu system of karatedo was developed in Japan proper in 1952 by Master Yamaguchi Gogen, a student of Okinawan master Miyagi Chojun. Master Yamaguchi, known as "The Cat," was one of the easiest karatedo masters for Westerners to recognize because of his trademark long hair, a rarity among Japanese Karatedo sensei. In addition Yamaguchi Sensei infused his karatedo style with his own spirituality, even creating a system he called Karate-Shinto, a mixture of ideas and practices taken from Shintoism, yoga, Zen, and karatedo. He was also fond of shamanistic practices, a favorite being to meditate beneath a waterfall. He felt that the drumming of the water on his head created a state of being which was conducive to spiritual awakening. The more ancient, shamanistic goal of the practice was to derive power from the energy-spirit (kami) of the waterfall.

Dojo of the Goju-ryu in Japan include the following:

Mr. Yamaguchi Hirofumi Goshi
International Karatedo Gojukai Association (IKGA)
34-10 Oyama-cho, Itabashi-ku, Tokyo 173-0023, Japan
Tel: (03) 974-5010
Fax: (03) 958-0670

Goju Ryu Karate-Do Gojukan
1-16-23 Zempukuji, Suginami-ku 167-0041 Tokyo, Japan
Tel: (03) 395-2311
Fax: (03) 390-2929

Japan Karatedo College
1-6-2 Zempukiji, Suginami-ku, Tokyo 167-0041, Japan

Mr. Michiro Noguchi
Etsukokai
Koshigaya-shi, Saitama-ken, Japan
e-mail: CXXO1536@niftyserve.or.jp

Kenshinkan Dojo
Nishitanabe-cho, Abeno-ku, Osaka-shi 545-0014 Japan
e-mail: ronbo@gol.com

Wado-ryu

Wado-ryu ("The Way of Peace") was founded in 1931 by Master Otsuka Hironori (1892–1982). When Master Funakoshi Gichin introduced Okinawan karatedo to Japan, Otsuka Sensei was a high-ranking exponent of Shindo Yoshin-ryu jujutsu. Funakoshi Sensei's demonstrations, teaching message, and style so affected Ohtsuka Sensei that he began the study of karatedo under the Okinawan master in 1922. By 1928 he was Funakoshi Sensei's assistant instructor and in 1931 Otsuka Sensei founded the Wado-ryu. Forty-one years later Otsuka Sensei received the title Shodai Karatedo Meijin Judan (First-Generation Karate Master of the Tenth Dan) from the Japanese imperial family. Otsuka Sensei was also presented the Shiju Hoshu medal for his outstanding contributions to physical education and sport from the government of Japan. Wado-ryu practitioners claim that Otsuka Sensei was the first master to create a karatedo style in the form of Japanese (not Okinawan) budo.

Wado-ryu karatedo is characterized by evasion instead of meeting force with force, and by light, fast, and fluid body movement. The Wado-ryu stylist defends with parries and deflections with simultaneous counterattacks.

The following are the Wado-ryu rules for practice; a listing of behaviors, by the way, that should be followed wherever one practices martial arts in Japan.

1. No idle chatter, smoking, alcohol, eating, chewing gum, etc. in the dojo.
2. All karateka must bow before entering and upon leaving the dojo. To those who practice karate the dojo is a sacred place. We

bow when entering the dojo to affirm our intention to train hard and seriously and we bow when leaving to show thanks for a good training session.

3. All karateka must bow to instructors or visiting instructors. We emphasis politeness at all times in the dojo and seek to cultivate a spirit based on gentleness and respect.

4. When the instructors or visiting instructors enter/exit the dojo, all karateka must stop whatever they are doing and face the sensei at the door and bow. Each person should seek to develop as full a state of attentiveness as possible. Karate requires and promotes a high degree of training of the mind as it does of the body.

5. A karate gi or loose comfortable clothing must be worn. No socks or shoes are permitted.

6. Show absolute obedience to your sensei. All instruction from the sensei or designated instructor must be followed.

7. Call your instructor "sensei."

8. Always acknowledge criticism given by the instructor or any other person. Respond to the sensei or a black belt instructor with the word "Hai!"

9. Never stand around with your hands on your waist. The standing position is the one assumed just before kata or yoi, namely two clenched fists in front of the body in standing position.

10. When sitting, always sit cross-legged or in seiza position.

11. Fingernails and toenails should be regularly cut in order to prevent injury.

12. Jewelry should not be worn in the dojo. It has no place in the dojo and can easily be broken or even cause injury.

13. In all practice, emphasis is placed on control, accuracy, and non-contact.

14. Do not attempt to learn or teach new forms without the expressed permission of the sensei.

15. The dojo is to be kept clean by all students. Please help to keep the floor dry, clean, and free of objects. Please look for a broom to sweep the floor as soon as you enter the dojo, before the start of class. Each student should do his or her part to contribute to a proper training environment.

16. If you arrive late, you must perform ten knuckle push-ups upon entering the dojo. Sit in seiza, bow once and stay seated until the sensei gives you permission to join in, or any other instructions. Then, bow again and proceed.
17. Report immediately to the sensei any injury or illness.
18. All karateka must stay inside the dojo. Inform the sensei if you must leave the dojo. Then follow the normal procedures for leaving the dojo.
19. Please check for all personal belongings before leaving the dojo.
20. Whatever you do, do it with all your might. Strengthen weak hands. Make your knees strong. Don't say "I'll work hard at a later time," etc. Practice a technique in the exact manner you'd apply it—with full force.
21. Each student is considered an integral part of the karate community. Should it become necessary to discontinue training for any reason, please notify the instructor. This is so that we may have an accurate and up-to-date record of all students.

Information concerning entrance into a Wado-ryu dojo in Japan may be obtained by contacting Mr. M. Furakawa, general secretary, in Tokyo. His telephone number is (0425) 91-3569. Fax: (0425) 91-3676.

Kyokushin

The founder of Kyokushin karatedo is Oyama Masutatsu Sosai. This style of karatedo is noted for its powerful techniques and emphasis on strength. Oyama Sensei, after all, killed a bull with his bare hands in order to make that point. The tenor of this style might be understood by considering Oyama Sensei's statement of "Kyokushin spirit": "Keep one's head low (modesty), eyes high (ambition), be reserved in speech (mind one's language) and kind in heart (treat others with respect and courtesy). Treat others with kindness; filial piety is the starting point (serve your parents well)." (from www.kyokushin.co.jp)

Oyama Sensei's eleven mottoes for karatedo training are as follows: (Ibid.)

1. The martial way begins and ends with courtesy.

2. Following the martial way is like scaling a cliff: continue upwards without rest.

3. Strive to seize the initiative in all things, all the time, guarding against actions stemming from selfish animosity or thoughtlessness.

4. Even for the martial artist, the place of money cannot be ignored. Yet one should be careful never to become attached to it.

5. The martial way is centered in posture. Strive to maintain correct posture at all times.

6. The martial way begins with one thousand days and is mastered after ten thousand days of training.

7. In the martial arts, introspection begets wisdom. Always see contemplation on your actions as an opportunity to improve.

8. The nature and purpose of the martial way is universal. All selfish desires should be roasted in the tempering fires of hard training.

9. The martial arts begin with a point and end in a circle. Straight lines stem from this principle.

10. The true essence of the martial way can only be realized through experience. Knowing this, learn never to fear its demands.

11. Always remember: in the martial arts the rewards of a confident and grateful heart are truly abundant.

The headquarters of the International Karate Organization (IKO), the organizational structure of Kyokushin Karatedo, can be contacted at the following address:

Matsui Shokei Kancho
International Karate Organization Kyokushinkaikan
2-38-1 Nishi Ikebukuro, Toshima-ku, Tokyo 171-0021, Japan

These are some of the many dojo in Japan (over four hundred as of last count) that teach the Kyokushin style of karatedo.

Mr. Hashizume Hidehiko
Kansai Hombu
2-5-9, Nakasaki, Kita-ku, Osaka-shi 530-0016, Japan
Tel: (06) 376-3703

Mr. Kamio Nobuyuki
Asakusa Dojo
Hanakawado Bldg. 1F, 1-3-6 Hanakawado, Taito-ku, Tokyo
111-0033, Japan. Tel: (03) 5828-5992. Fax: (813) 5828-5925

Mr. Kamio Nobuyuki
Kanda Dojo
108 Tokyo Bldg. 8F, 3-20-6 Uchi Kanda, Chiyoda-ku, Tokyo
101-0047, Japan. Tel: (03) 5294-6633

Mr. Sugimura Taichiro
Yotsuya Dojo
Yamaichi Bldg. BF, 3-11 Yotsuya, Shinjuku-ku, Tokyo
160-0004, Japan. Tel: (03) 3357-8555

Mr. Shokei Matsui
Sapporo Dojo
Nakanoshima Com-Square Bldg. 7F, 1-7-20,
Nakanoshima, Toyohira-ku, Sapporo-shi 062-0921, Japan
Tel: (01) 816-3939

Mr. Yokoyama Makoto
Hakodate Branch Dojo
98-192 Jinkawa-cho, Hakodate-shi, Hokkaido 041-0833, Japan
Tel: (13) 854-8199

Mr. Sekikawa Hiroaki
Niigata Branch Dojo
1-7-1 Nishikoharidai, Niigata-shi 950-2012, Japan
Tel: (25) 268-3490

Mr. Ito Kazuma
Akita Branch Dojo
45 Numabukuro-aza, Matsubuchi, Kawabe-machi, Kawabe-gun,
Akita-ken 019-2613, Japan Tel: 81188-82-3395

Mr. Hamai Yoshiaki
Toyama Branch Dojo
6-40 Akebono-cho, Toyama-shi, Toyama-ken 930-0847, Japan
Tel: (76) 433-6678

Mr. Kawabata Koichi
Kyoto Branch Dojo
Nuiville Ninsei 4F, 23 Ninsei Shogo-cho, Chukyo-ku,
Kyoto-shi 604-8812, Japan. Tel: (75) 321-1956

Mr. Hata Takanori
Nara Branch Dojo
Excellence Bldg. 1F, 3-1-33 Omiya-cho, Nara-shi 630-8115, Japan
Tel: (74) 233-5799

Mr. Masaki Takao
Osaka East Branch Dojo
2-3-13 Egeyama-cho, Hyogo-ku, Kobe-shi, 652-0043, Japan
Tel: (90) 8456-3399

Mr. Takami Nariaki
Ehime Branch Dojo
3-10-1, Nagahori, Uwajima-shi, Ehime-ken 798-0082, Japan
Tel: (89) 522-7497

Mr. Abe Kiyofumi
Fukuoka Dojo
Kouyou Bldg. 2F, 15-16, Tamagawa-cho, Minami-ku,
Fukuoka-shi 815-0037, Japan. Tel: (92) 553-6807

Shorinji Kempo

Shorinji Kempo (Shaolin Temple Fist Method) was created by its founder So Doshin in the 1940s in Tadotsu, Japan. Shorinji Kempo, perhaps more than the other styles discussed so far, looks to China for its inspiration. The founder studied martial arts in China for seventeen years while working as an operative of the Japanese government, and upon returning home combined them with Japanese fighting arts to form an empty-handed fighting style that bears a superficial resemblance to a combination of karatedo and aikido.

So Doshin's inspiration was the mind and body training methods of the monks of the Shaolin temple, while the direct instigation to his creation of Shorinji Kempo was the disastrous state of Japanese society after World War II. So Doshin created Shorinji Kempo to help the Japanese, especially young people, to develop the spirit and strength of mind and body to enable them to rebuild a new and better Japanese society.

Shorinji Kempo is a registered religion in Japan. This came about in the aftermath of World War II when, for obvious reasons, the Occupation forces banned the study of martial arts. However, a variety of new religions sprang up from the ashes of Japanese defeat, one of which was a "dancing religion." So Doshin argued that if such a thing was tolerated, then why not a "fighting religion"? He won his point. The British forces on Shikoku even allowed the Shorinji Kempo group to use its boxing ring, gloves, and training facilities. The "religious" coloration of Shorinji Kempo must not be seen in the Western sense of a system of worship of a supreme being, but rather in a more Asian sense of a code of life, a "Way."

Shorinji Kempo stresses the following basic principles (from www.shorinjikempo.or.jp/wsko/guide.html):

1. Ken zen ichinyo (body and mind are the same). Zen refers to the spirit. Ken to the body. Students of Shorinji Kempo should seek to develop both body and mind.
2. Riki ai funi (strength and love stand together). Strength supported by love, and love supported by strength. The condition in which the two apparent opposites are unified as one, is what a man's way of thinking and acting should have as the core.
3. Shushu koju (defend first, attack after). Shorinji Kempo is a method of self-defense. It begins with defense, not with attack.
4. Kumite shutai (pair work is fundamental). In Shorinji Kempo training there are two roles: an attacker's and a defender's. Cooperation among the two is the most important requirement for learning.
5. Fusatsu Katsujin (protect people without injury). Never seek a fight. Protect yourself. Hurting people is not the purpose of training in Shorinji Kempo.

For information concerning training in Shorinji Kempo while in Japan, you may write the Headquarters at the following address:

World Shorinji Kempo Organization
3-1, Tadotsu-cho
Nakatado-gun
Kagawa-ken 764-8511
Japan

Judo: The Gentle Way

Judo, an Olympic sport as well as a way of life for its thousands of practitioners worldwide, was the creation of Professor Kano Jigoro (1860–1936). As a young man, Kano Sensei traveled Japan, studying jujutsu (systems of unarmed combat) with some of the finest instructors available. Jujutsu, some say, was introduced into Japan in the seventeenth century by a Chinese master named Ching-Ping. Again, as we have seen in discussing the schools of karatedo, it is typical of Japanese traditional culture to revere Chinese arts and claim that in some way China was the source of the arts of Japan. There is no doubt some truth in that, but it is also true that the Japanese did not sit around defenseless until the Chinese showed up to teach them how to fight. The very earliest Chinese documents concerning contact with the Japanese describe the Japanese warriors as formidable characters.

Jujutsu is characterized by attacks against joints of the body that are intended to break and cripple and by throwing and pinning techniques. It was a form of fighting that the samurai learned as an adjunct to their weapons studies. Unarmed methods of fighting became even more significant after the Meiji Restoration of 1868, and especially after 1876, when wearing of swords in public was forbidden. Kano Sensei was not merely a martial arts enthusiast, he was first and foremost an educator. It was Professor Kano who personally influenced much of the physical education program of the newly structured Japanese educational system. He sifted through the techniques of jujutsu, saved the ones that could be practiced safely, added some elements, and formed his "new" art as a sport for the physical education program in the Japanese school system. As with the founders of many Japanese martial arts, Kano Sensei was interested in providing, especially for the youth of Japan, a method of education that would serve the physical, mental, and spiritual health needed to maintain a vigorous and forward-looking Japanese society.

Professor Kano established the world headquarters of judo, the Kodokan, in Tokyo in 1882 and proceeded to codify rules of tournament competition still found in modern judo. In 1909 Kano Sensei became the first Asian member of the International Olympic Committee. One of his dreams was realized in 1964 when judo became an official event in the Olympic Games.

For Westerners who want to practice judo in Japan, the Kodokan International Judo Center in Tokyo is the place to go, both to train and to learn the location of certified *judojo* in other cities in Japan. An eight-story building, the Kodokan International Judo Center was dedicated in 1984 in commemoration of the hundredth anniversary of the founding of the Kodokan. This facility is the most elaborate martial arts training facility in all Japan, beginning with the lodging it provides for visiting *judoka*.

On the third floor of the Kodokan International Judo Center are five large rooms, each housing twenty individuals. There are also private rooms. Lodging fees (per person, for one night) as of 1999 were as follows:

Training camp room: ¥1,800
Single room: ¥3,500
Deluxe single room: ¥5,000
Deluxe twin room: ¥9,000
Extra bed: ¥1,800

On the second floor of the center are the Kano Memorial Hall, Historical Hall, and exhibition room. Here one can see photographs, documents, awards, and letters from various distinguished individuals related to the history of judo. The second floor also houses the library, with over seven thousand books on the many facets of judo. The center also supports research facilities centered in four main areas: theoretical and historical study of judo, the psychological study of judo, the technical analysis of judo, research on the physical strength of judo practitioners, and the physiological study of judo.

There is a shop selling Kodokan judo goods, with items ranging from "Shihan Special Calendars" for ¥1,050 and judo neckties for ¥3,675 to Kodokan bath towels in a variety of colors for ¥1,050. The Kodokan Judo Video Series is available with prices ranging between three and seven thousand yen. Yen-dollar exchange rates vary but may be checked through local banks or online. Authorized books on judo as well as copies of the *Bulletin of the Association for the Scientific Study of Judo* are also obtainable at the center shop in price ranges from three to seven thousand yen. You can contact the Kodokan Internet Shop, the official store of the Kodokan Center, at:

Yuko Takeuchi
Kodokan Internet Shop
1-35-28-1209 Hongo, Bunkyo-ku
Tokyo 113
Tel: (03) 5803-2825
e-mail: kshop@tk.hint.co.jp

The Kodokan Center has a vast practice area divided into a number of dojo spaces. The Main Dojo is on the seventh floor: it measures 420 mats (each approximately three by six feet) in area, with seating for nine hundred spectators. This is where official judo tournament events are held. The Main Dojo may be rented for ¥200,000 a day.

The School Dojo is 420 mats and can be divided into two rooms if necessary. Rental fee: ¥50,000 per day; ¥40,000 for a half day (morning or evening). The International Dojo is 192 mats. Rental fee: ¥30,000 per day; ¥20,000 for a half day (morning or evening). The Women's Dojo is 240 mats and can be divided into two rooms. Rental fee: ¥50,000 per day; ¥40,000 for a half day (morning or evening). The Boy's Dojo is 114 mats. Rental fee: ¥30,000 per day; ¥20,000 for a half day (morning or evening). The Special Dojo is for retired *judo-ka* and for those who are doing various sorts of research on judo techniques.

At the Kodokan Center, there is an Adult Division, a Women's Division, and an International Division for *judoka* from outside Japan. The Adult Division practices between 3:30 p.m. and 8:00 p.m. on weekdays; on Saturday practices are held between 4:00 and 7:30. In the Adult Division instruction is led by a team of four instructors with experience in championship competition. The Women's Division practices at the Center between 5:30 and 7:30 p.m., and the International Division practices throughout the day from Monday through Saturday. The International Division is divided into two levels. Class B is composed of *judoka* from beginner levels to second *kyu*, while Class A is for those ranking first *kyu* and above.

Fees for practicing at the Kodokan Center, as of 1999, are as follows:

Boys' Division: admission, ¥ 6,000; entrance fee, ¥6,000; tuition, ¥5,000; member's card ¥500. Total: ¥17,500 yen.

Adult Division (men and women): admission, ¥6,000; entrance fee, ¥1000; tuition, ¥5,000; member's card, ¥500. Total: ¥12,500.

International Division: admission, ¥ 6,000; entrance fee, ¥6,000; tuition, ¥5,000; member's card ¥500. Total: ¥17,500 yen.

Kodokan Judo Headquarters is located at:
1-16-30 Kasuga, Bunkyo-ku, Tokyo 112, Japan.

For English-speaking services (practice times, locations, fees, lodging facilities for *judoka* from overseas) contact:

Kodokan School of Judo, Department of International Affairs
Tel: (03) 3818-4172 Fax: (03) 3814-2918
e-mail: int-kdn@po.iijnet.or.jp

If you will be located in the Osaka area, contact:

Kodokan Osaka International Judo Center
4-15-11 Nagata, Joto-ku, Osaka, Japan
Tel: (06) 961-0640

Judo is my favorite way for children to enter the martial arts. Most children would love to spend an hour or so wrestling with one another in baggy clothes on a soft gymnastic floor. If you will be with your children while in Japan you might look into a nearby children's judo club. I found that most Japanese parents who seek to expose their children to martial arts at a young age will select either judo or kendo. It was very common in the area in which I lived to see young children late in the afternoon with blue bags of kendo armor or *judogi* riding the subway to their martial arts class. Judo, a very popular sport in Japan, also appeals to the teenagers and young adults. Some of the most ferocious competition takes place at the high school and college levels.

I cannot recommend judo for middle-aged people who are not in excellent physical condition, or for senior citizens. The crashing break-falls typical of judo take their toll on the body over time, having a particular deleterious effect on knee joints. I have heard of judo classes for senior citizens but I have never seen one. Many wounded former *judoka* find their way into aikido, in which the fundamental principles of judo still apply but violence to the body is much less. Before arthroscopic surgery, retired *judo* players could be easily identified by three- and four-inch scars around their knees. However, if you do happen to meet a high-ranked middle-aged or elderly *judoka* on the mat, thank him or her ahead of time for the lesson he or she is about to teach you.

When I was training in jodo at the Fukuoka Budokan, the Olympics were being held in Korea. Several foreign judo clubs stopped there to warm up with the Fukuoka Budokan judo club before moving on to Seoul for the main events. The physical preparation for the technical teaching in a judo class is awe-inspiring. Some of the heavyweights in the budokan would hoist their partners on their backs and run up and down the steps in the bleachers, after which they would perform a hundred push-ups—with their partners still on their backs. Then came the wind sprints. And on and on.

The largely middle-aged *jodoka* (practitioners of the way of the short staff) while practicing their stately war dance with sword and staff on another part of the Budokan practice floor, would furrow their brows and smile with a look on their face that said, "Those boys must be crazy," every time the floor trembled from the force of a two-hundred-pound *judoka* being driven to the mat by his sparring partner.

As the Olympic frenzy died down, however, the Fukuoka Budokan judo club subtly changed back to its normal tempo. One typical evening after my jodo class, I watched the judo players work out. A father sat on the sidelines coaching his daughter as hard as he could (with his facial expressions) while eight feet away his ten-year-old darling was being introduced to a hip throw, an often frightening prospect for beginners. The judo sensei, on one knee with his hand lightly touching the little girl's elbow, urging her to *gambatte!* (try hard; put up a good fight) was teaching the little girl to overcome her fear. She, though knowing her father was nearby, never took her eyes off the sensei. The senior student who was selected to throw the little girl knew his part and was obviously pleased that his sensei had trusted him enough to select him for this subtle and crucial moment. There was a palpable sense of kinship among the four. It was as if the sensei, the father, the daughter, and the senior student were all related.

Meanwhile, the heavyweights formed a territory of their own on the dojo floor. Serious young judo competitors are some of the largest, strongest, and fastest martial artists I saw while living in Japan. At the same time several elderly, white-haired men with low-slung black belts floated among the various components of the class, visiting, answering questions, and demonstrating, after which those they engaged would bow very deeply as the elders completed their instructions and moved on. On another part of the judo floor earnest senior students taught basic throws to the beginners. The pattern of practice had a feeling of the eternal.

Kendo: The Way of the Sword

The signature weapon of the samurai was the sword. It was everything to the warrior and has been called the soul of the samurai.
Swordsmanship, as opposed to mere hacking away at an enemy with
a bladed weapon, dates to as early as 789 A.D., when kumitachi
(sword exercises) were used in the instruction of the sons of the kuge
(noblemen) at the court in Nara. Its roots no doubt go back ever far-
ther, perhaps even a thousand years earlier.

Many legendary swordsmen range across the history of Japan. The
warrior-monk Saito Musashi-bo Benkei (d. 1190) swore to take a
thousand swords in combat, and almost made it until he came to the
last one he needed. It was in the hands of Minamoto Yoshitsune. After
Yoshitsume defeated Benkei, the monk became his chief retainer. The
story of these two is very similar to the English tale of Robin Hood
and Little John. Yoshitsune's exceptional swordsmanship was, the
story goes, taught to him by the *tengu*, mythological beings that
looked like a cross between a bird and a goblin, who lived on Mount
Hiei near Kyoto. Many later sword schools attempted to obtain prestige by linking the origins of their style to Yoshitsune.

History also tells of Tsukahara Bokuden, a lord from eastern Japan
who mastered the sword arts taught at the Kashima shrine. He fought

nineteen times with the live blade, man to man, took part in thirty-seven regular battles, and fought several hundred *bokken* (wooden sword) matches. He died in 1571 at the age of eighty. During his long life he reportedly killed more than two hundred of his enemies. He received six battle wounds during his career, all from arrows (Williams, 1975: 21ff).

Perhaps the most famous of all Japanese swordsmen was Miyamoto Musashi, called *kensei* (sword saint). A fantastic character, Musashi fought over eighty duels with live blades and remained undefeated. In an epic battle on a small island between Kyushu and Honshu, the great Musashi killed his nemesis Sasaki Kojiro with a single blow from a *bokken*. He had whittled the makeshift sword out of an old boat oar he had begged from the fisherman who was ferrying him to the island where the duel with Kojiro was to take place, ostensibly because he had overslept the morning of the duel and rushed off without his swords.

Musashi was not only a swordfighter. He also gained renown as a painter, sculptor, and designer of children's toys. In his later years he wrote *Gorin no Sho* (The Book of Five Rings), considered one of the key books about *heiho* (tactics) in the Japanese martial arts. Musashi created the Nito-ryu, a two-sword style of fencing made easy for him by the fact that he was ambidextrous.

Modern kendo is derived from the inspiration of the great swordsmen and modified by the Japanese social structure and cultural norms that became current during the Tokugawa period (1600–1868). In the later years of the era a practice weapon called the *shinai* came into common usage as a surrogate sword to enable the sword students to strike hard at each other without doing the damage which could result from a *katana* (live blade) or a *bokken*. About four feet long, the *shinai* is made of four strips of bamboo bound together to form a flexible, hollow cylinder that, equipped with a *tsuba* (hand guard) and a leather-wrapped grip, completes the image of the war sword. A red cord is stretched from the handle to the tip of the *shinai* to give a blade-edge focus to the weapon. In fact, the "edge of the blade" is on the opposite side of the *shinai* from the red cord. In tournaments a valid strike is called when a player strikes his or her opponent in a prescribed area with the top third of the *shinai* on the side opposite the cord.

The *shinai*, due to its flexible "give," cannot break bones, but can leave nasty bruises. To minimize injury, *kendoka* wear *bogu* (protective gear) composed of a *tare* (a kind of protective apron), a *do* (breastplate), *kote* (fencing gloves), and a *men* (face mask). *Bogu* are worn over a *dogi* and *hakama*, both of which are traditionally blue.

In *shiai-geiko* (competitive matches) a valid point is scored when the *kendoka* identifies the target on his/her opponent fractions of a second before he/she strikes. There are four target points: *men* (cut to the head), *kote* (cut to the wrist), *do* (cut across the abdomen), and *tsuki* (thrust to the throat). Listening to the fighters call their targets gives a running commentary on what is happening. At a Kendo match, one hears the opponents shouting *"Men! Men! Kote! Do! Men! Men!"*

Kendo also has a series of *kata* (choreographed fighting moves) that are executed with *bokken* by two *kendoka*. The first seven of these exercises feature long sword against long sword, while the last three illustrate the use of the short sword against the long sword. More advanced kendo *kata* find live blades being used.

Despite the bloody history of the sword arts and the intense practice of competitive fighting in kendo, it remains a budo and as such focuses on loftier goals than merely beating up on someone at a competitive match. For *kendoka* worldwide the following is understood as the purpose of kendo practice (from www.kendo-usa.org/creed.htm):

To mold the mind and body,
To cultivate a vigorous spirit,
And through correct and rigid training,
To strive for improvement in the art of kendo;
To hold in esteem human courtesy and honor,
To associate with others with sincerity,
And to forever pursue the cultivation of oneself.
Thus will one be able to love his country and society,
To contribute to the development of culture,
And to promote peace and prosperity among all people.

As noted, kendo, like judo, is an excellent choice for children just starting out in the martial arts. The ample protective gear worn by *kendoka* gives adequate protection from serious injury. The controlled rough-and-tumble "sword" fight, while dressed in stylized armor, is fun for practitioners of all ages.

Judo is great for kids and younger adults, but tends to lose many of its serious players in later middle age, while kendo can be practiced safely by people of all ages. The kendo sensei who taught my sons was in his late sixties. He rarely wore armor when he fenced with his senior students, and could outmaneuver even the fastest of them. All proponents of the Japanese martial arts should at least once in their life fight in armor. It is humbling.

An image of kendo that remains strong in my memory was generated during the ceremonies of Taiiku no Hi (Sports Day). All practitioners at the Fukuoka Budokan were invited to demonstrate their arts on the grounds of Gokoku Jinja, a large Shinto shrine in Fukuoka. The atmosphere of the event was joyous and celebratory. Several martial arts performers at a time offered their demonstrations before a knowledgeable and appreciative audience. It was during this time that I was asked to perform aikido techniques as part of the Gokokuji Aikidojo demonstration. This invitation was not, I am sure, due to my expertise in aikido, but because the aikido sensei knew that I would be thrilled, as well as challenged, to perform my aikido *waza* before the "hometown" crowd, as it were. Likewise, since *gaijin* (foreigners) were rare in the martial arts of Fukuoka, it was interesting for the local audiences to watch one perform.

After our dojo had completed its demonstration I spent the rest of the afternoon strolling the temple grounds enjoying the demonstrations. I watched as the *jukendoka* (students of the bayonet), one of the roughest looking martial arts I saw while in Japan, sparred. Next to them an *aiki jujutsu* club showed some unique training *kata*. The high point for me, however, was the demonstration of the kendo clubs.

At one point, the *kendoka* arrayed themselves into about a dozen sparring pairs and took up positions spaced evenly throughout an area about half the size of a football field. At a command, these groups fought and the judges watched. Overhead banners snapped in the wind and the shouts of the swordfighters and the clashing of weapons and armor filled the air, which turned golden as the sunlight pierced the clouds of dust. Standing in the midst of armored swordfighters as they clash, shout *kiai,* and clash again, was one of the emotional peaks of my time in Japan.

Another thing that was made abundantly clear in the Taiiku no Hi celebrations was that the various demonstrations of the budokan were intended as a kind of prayer. It is no accident that the event was held on the grounds of a Shinto shrine as opposed to a budokan or an open field in a local park. The sincere energy expended by the budo-ka is offered as a prayer for protection. The shrine's name translates as "Shrine for Defense of the Nation." It would be like a Western martial arts group performing a spirited demonstration in the sanctuary of a church. Westerners may find such an event disrespectful, but such an attitude simply shows a lack of understanding of cultural differences. In Japan martial arts may be seen as a kind of spiritual offering or prayer, sometimes more so than others.

To inquire about kendo practice in Japan, contact either of the following:

International Kendo Federation (IKF)
c/o Nippon Budokan
2-3 Kitanomaru Koen, Chiyoda-ku, Tokyo 102-0091, Japan
Tel: (03) 3211-5804
Fax: (03) 3211-5807

Zen Nippon Kendo Renmei (ZNKR)
c/o Nippon Budokan -0091
2-3 Kitanomaru Koen, Chiyoda-ku, Tokyo 102, Japan

Kyudo: The Way of the Bow

One of the earliest Japanese designations of a warrior life was "the way of the bow and the horse." Siddhartha Gautama, the Buddha, as noted previously, won his bride because of his success in an archery contest. A bow is wielded in a brief kata by victorious sumo wrestlers. In ancient China, the imperial orchestra was tuned by thumping the strings of bows of various lengths. Every twenty years the Ise shrine, the most sacred in Japan, is ritually cleansed and reconstructed, and Goshinpo Yumi (sacred bows) are used in the rededication. Bows and arrows are also found in rituals surrounding childbirth and in Boys Day and Coming-of-Age Day rituals. It is an old Japanese folk-belief that the "twang" of a bowstring drives away evil spirits.

The bow was important from the very beginning in Japan. The Jomon period (beginning about five to seven thousand years ago) was the time of hunting and gathering people who used a variety of bows in hunting and warfare. In the succeeding Yayoi period (300 B.C.–A.D. 300) the bow became a symbol of political power. Japan's first Emperor, Jimmu (660 B.C.), is always depicted holding a bow in paintings. In the *Accounts of the Three Kingdoms* (A.D. 297) Chinese envoys offer the first description of the asymmetrical bow (two-thirds of the length above the handgrip and one-third below) that is still used in modern kyudo.

Sometime between 330 and 1192, the Japanese, extending their own bow-making technology and borrowing some techniques from China, began to construct what is now the standard kyudo bow. Rather than being made of a single piece of wood, it was a sophisticated composite made of carefully fitted and glued strips of hard and soft woods and bamboo. Besides being asymmetrical it is also one of the longer bows used in the world. The one I shot in Japan was over seven feet long. The traditional kyudo *yumi* (bow) is still made in Japan, but it is rightfully acknowledged as a work of art as well as a weapon, and will cost several thousand dollars. Bows made of synthetic materials which imitate the bamboo bows in weight and shape, if not feel, will cost several hundred dollars.

I asked my kyudo sensei, Asakuma Shihan, why the kyudo bow was asymmetrical. Her teacher had told her that the bow was designed for horsemen. Since most of the length was above the grip, the horseman's bow would extend only minimally downward where it would be less likely to be jostled or grabbed in combat by enemies on the ground. I also asked her why the *kyudoka* carries only two arrows in formal shooting *kata*. Her answer again stemmed from her teacher and found explanation in the reality of ancient warfare. She noted that an archer could get only two shots off at an enemy charging on horseback from a distance of twenty-eight meters (a standard kyudo shooting distance).

By the late twelfth century there were many schools of *kyujutsu* (military archery). Heki Danjo Masatsugu (1443–1502), founder of the Heki-ryu *kyujutsu*, contributed to the perpetuation of archery in Japan by standardizing archery training techniques. However, the end of military archery came in 1575 when Oda Nobunaga commanded a conscript force of musketeers against an opposing force of archers. The archers, of course, fared badly against the guns.

Beginning in the time of peace brought about by the Tokugawa shogunate in the seventeenth century, archery slowly evolved from *kyujutsu* to kyudo. For many, the practice of archery ceased to be associated with killing the enemy and became more attuned to personal development. A key actor in this transition was Honda Toshizane, an archery instructor at Tokyo Imperial University in the early twentieth century who combined facets of ceremonial and military archery to form Honda-ryu kyudo. Although there were complaints from the military schools and the ceremonial systems, most authorities credit Honda Toshizane with the creation of modern kyudo. In 1949 the Zen Nihon Kyudo Renmei (All Japan Kyudo Federation) was established to regulate kyudo and in 1953 this organization published the *Kyudo Kyohon* (manual of basic kyudo shooting procedures) that is still the basis of kyudo practice in most of Japan.

I could discern perhaps three broad types of Japanese kyudo practitioners. The high school and college students who shot as a sport were on one end, and those who practiced the Zen of archery were on the other, with most everyone else somewhere between these two poles. The adults with whom I practiced kyudo approached it as a study of the harmony, beauty, and order that can be found in the serious study of any activity—making tea, arranging flowers, or shooting an arrow—the perfection of the authentic act. They also really wanted to hit the target. I can vividly remember my kyudo *sempai* preparing for her fourth-degree black belt test, in which hitting the target with both arrows is mandatory. When she missed with both, she screwed up her eyes, lifted her face toward the ceiling, and rocked back and forth on her heels, a study in frustration. Hardly Zen-like, but very human.

I found that some Japanese archery clubs (not kyudo groups) are purely Western and "sport" oriented. They use sophisticated compound bows made of various synthetic materials instead of the traditional bamboo longbows, and dress in Western sports clothes with team logos on hats and jackets instead of wearing the *dogi* and *hakama* worn by the *kyudoka*. They value the numerical scoring in shooting competition in lieu of the great emphasis placed on the display of proper form in kyudo.

Kyudo can be enjoyed by people of all ages. The basic physical requirement for comfortable kyudo practice is the ability to kneel and stand without using your hands to push off the floor. You will do this about forty times in a period of an hour or more. The bow is selected to fit the strength of the student and therefore provide minimum strain in the upper body and arms. The difficulty in the practice of kyudo is maintaining the mental focus required to shoot accurately while performing within the classical form. The solitary nature of kyudo practice and the mental discipline required make kyudo an excellent form of meditation. The book *Zen and the Art of Archery* by Eugene Herrigel (New York: Pantheon Books, 1953) was recommended by Asakuma Shihan as a necessary text for Westerners to gain some understanding of archery at the level at which she practiced.

I remember one spring evening when many archers had come to the dojo where men, women, and children of all ages happily visited with one another. Occasionally individuals would break away for a few solemn moments, select two arrows, and with bow in one hand and arrows in the other, grandly enter the shooting area, every step and turn preordained in the basic shooting *kata*. After the austere act of shooting, they continued visiting with neighbors and friends.

The contrast between the friendly banter and laughter as the dojo mates awaited their turn to shoot, and the deeply solemn nature of the act of shooting, seemed appropriate to the entire fabric I came to see and feel in kyudo. It is hard to explain and maybe cannot be rationally conveyed, but I felt that the preshooting behavior with its casual air of a good time spent with friends complemented the deep seriousness of actually shooting the arrows. It was as if a deep-structure yin/yang informed the nature of the students' behavior. Each shot was somehow a gift to the perpetuation of the community's harmony, a labor of compassion, support for the group, and a celebration.

Kyudo clubs are quite common in Japan. Check at the nearest budokan. Generally the fee you pay allows the use of the club's bows and arrows. The bows used by the clubs are usually fiberglass with nylon strings but are built to the specifications of the traditional bamboo war bow. You will quickly outgrow the club's arrows and will want to buy your own custom-made ones, an expensive but worthwhile proposition. Due to my height (six feet, four inches) and my long arms, my customized arrows were huge compared to the standard arrows used by the Japanese *kyudoka*. I felt like I was shooting telephone poles! My *kyudojo* mates found the length of my arrows, which were almost twice the size of the standard arrows used by my fellow students, a constant source of amusement.

Kyudojo members often bring antique bamboo bows and arrows to practice. This is a time for even more informal conversation and appreciation and is often the time when the sensei, as he or she examines the antique bow, offers important information about kyudo, bow makers, local dojo history, and customs.

Kyudo clubs, like most other martial arts clubs, have a full schedule of dojo parties, tournament trips, holiday gatherings, and special seminars during which the students and teachers bond with each other. During these times teachers may make themselves more accessible to students' questions than in a formal dojo setting.

Kyudo is an excellent martial art for those interested in a meditative and cultural-historical experience of subtle profundity. To face the target, bow and arrows in hand, is to be wonderfully alone and to experience the truth of who you are at the moment you let the arrow fly. Kyudo feels regal and stately and takes you to an ancient place. There is something seductive about that infinite moment when the arrow is rushing toward the target and you wait. It is one of the most expanded fractions of a second you will ever experience. Asakuma Shihan told me through an interpreter that it took a long, long time for the arrow to hit the target.

The sounds of kyudo are an important part of the enjoyment of the art. The "thruumm" of the bowstring, as I noted earlier, was believed to have a power all its own. Likewise, the sound of the arrow hitting (or missing) the target carries its own information. Most of the time I heard the soft, mushy "thunk" when my arrows missed the target and hit the bank of black sand against which the *mato* (targets) were set. When the target is hit, a better sound happens. If you hit the *mato* (which resembles a large tambourine) near the edge, you hear a relatively high-pitched drum beat. The sound that is most wonderful, however, is the deep "boom" of a target being struck dead center. Normally, as her students shot, Asakuma Shihan would sit on a quilt on the floor drinking tea with her friends, her back to the students. However, when any one of us managed to produce the deep "boom" of a bull's-eye, Asakuma Shihan would, without turning to see who had hit the target, lift her little cup of tea in salute, a delighted smile on her face.

Usually only once during a training session would Asakuma Shihan pick up her bow and arrow to shoot. When that happened the students immediately took off their shooting gloves and hurried onto the dojo floor to sit formally as the *shihan* demonstrated the Zen of archery. At these moments I was always struck with how this diminutive woman seemed to grow in size as she carried her bow and arrows to the shooting line. Her gaze as she looked down the range at the target was of the utmost intensity. There seemed to be a quietness around her, a kind of spiritual gravity—and she almost always hit the target with both arrows!

When I was her student, Asakuma Shihan was ranked as an eighth-degree black belt by the Zen Nippon Kyudo Renmei. To understand what that means, the following, drawn from the *Kyudo Kyohon* (volume 1, pp. 201-202), lists the requirements for kyudo ranking and it is worth pointing out that the requirements and expectations for various rank in kyudo are approximately the same for all Japanese budo:

Rank Requirements

Third *kyu* : One who is judged able to both perform the basic movements of shooting and handling the equipment to a certain degree, showing that he or she is training under systematic instruction.

Second *kyu*: One who is judged to have made marked improvement over the third *kyu* level of training.

First *kyu:* One whose shooting form (*shaho hassetsu*) and conduct of shooting (*taihai*) are judged to be correct in their main points.

First *dan*: One whose shooting form and *taihai* conform to the proper form and who has reached a level where the arrow flight is consistent and not erratic.

Second *dan* : One whose shooting form and *taihai* both show proper form, whose execution of shooting techniques shows vitality and spirit, and whose arrow flight is consistent and not erratic.

Third *dan*: One whose form has developed consistency, whose *taihai* has become settled and calm, whose breathing is well regulated, whose execution of shooting technique follows the correct principles, and whose arrows fly straight and with fairly consistent accuracy.

Fourth *dan*: One who, in addition to the required elements for third *dan*, has correct breathing, a sharp *hanare* (release of arrow), and has reached a level where accuracy is consistent.

Fifth *dan*: One whose shooting form, shooting technique, and taihai all conform to correct principles, who has begun to display *shahin* (dignity, quality, and elegance in shooting), and who, in particular, is judged to have achieved refinement.

Sixth *dan:* One who shows excellent shooting technique and whose further development of refinement is striking and obvious.

Seventh *dan:* One who has made shooting form, shooting technique, and *taihai* a part of him or herself so that they are naturally expressed, who is possessed of a high degree of *shahin*, and who has reached an expert level.

Eighth *dan:* One whose technical ability is perfect (mature), whose *shahin* is refined and elegant, and who has mastered the mysteries of the art of shooting.

Ninth *dan*: One who has penetrated to the ultimate truth of kyudo.

Tenth *dan:* AUTHOR'S NOTE: This rank is posthumously awarded, or reserved for the headmaster of a *ryu*.

The spirit of kyudo may be further ascertained by considering the *Shahokun* (Principles of Shooting) by Master Yoshimi Junsei (from www.asahi-net.or.jp/~nf3m-ootk/shahokun.html):

> The Way is not with the bow, but with the bone, which is of the greatest importance in shooting. Placing Spirit (kokoro) in the center of the whole body, with two-thirds of the yunde (left arm) push the string, and with one-third of the mete (right arm) pull the bow. Spirit settled, this becomes harmonious unity. From the center line of the chest, divide the left and right equally into release. It is written, that the collision of iron and stone will release sudden sparks; and thus there is the golden body, shining white, and the half moon positioned in the west.

The *Raiki Shagi* (Record of Etiquette, Truth of Shooting) also offers ancient advice to the *kyudoka:*

> The shooting, with the round of moving forward or backward, can never be without courtesy and propriety. After having acquired the

right inner intention and correctness in the outward appearance, the bow and arrow can be handled resolutely. To shoot in this way is to perform the shooting with success, and through this shooting virtue will be evident. Kyudo is the way of perfect virtue. In the shooting, one must search for rightness in oneself. With the rightness of self, shooting can be realized. At the time when shooting fails, there should be no resentment toward those who win. On the contrary, this is an occasion to search for oneself.

Whenever I think of kyudo, a feeling of beauty arises in me. Budo training is not only, or merely, about weapons and defeating enemies. When my arrow managed to strike the *mato* (target), I understood vaguely, and as an historical footnote, that I had just successfully put an arrow into an attacker's chest. But even that act was far more about the elegance of performing the act as opposed to some acknowledgment that if a warrior were charging me across an open space, I would have killed him. There is beauty and power in the flight of an arrow, in the friendship and affection of members of the dojo, and in a variety of events that one experiences as part of a martial arts dojo in Japan. For example, the Japanese celebrate November 3 as Culture Day (Bunka no Hi). The day is about peace, freedom, advancement of culture, and awards and acknowledgment for artistic achievement. Since budo is comparable to what the West calls fine arts, the members of many budojo in Fukuoka gather to take part in the Culture Day celebrations.

When I took part, the staging area for the martial arts contingents was the castle grounds. We were to march down from the castle and order our ranks in a small valley at the foot of the castle mound where the city dignitaries and audience awaited. The day was crisp and cool. Leaves of gingko and maple covered the ground with splashes of yellow, gold, and scarlet. Hundreds of *budojo* arranged themselves in marching order. The archers carried their bows and arrows; the staff fighters, their *bo* and the *jo*. Kendo clubs arrived in their armor, and the various karate dojo and judo clubs gleamed in their crisp white *dogi*. Several naginata dojo, carrying their long weapons, some of their members dressed in armor, lined up behind the *jukendo* (bayonet fighter) contingent. There were also spear fighters. The iaido clubs dressed in fancy kimono and *hakama* and marched carrying their swords slung in their *obi*. Several hundred budo students marched together through the complex network of walled paths that delineated the middle grounds of the castle. I could almost hear and see the samurai of Lord Kuroda who once rode out of this castle. As far as I could see both before and behind me were martial artists arrayed against the backdrop of the castle. I felt as if I were part of a Kurosawa film, a sensation that would recur during my time in Japan.

To inquire concerning kyudojo in which you may train while in Japan, contact:

Zen Nippon Kyudo Renmei
Kishi Memorial Hall
1-1-1 Jinnan, Shibuya-ku, Tokyo 150-0041, Japan

Aikido: The Way of Harmony

As with all Japanese martial arts, aikido claims an illustrious beginning and a singularly dramatic development. Its roots reach back to at
least the ninth century, when oral tradition has it that Prince
Sadazumi (874–916), the son of Emperor Seiwa, observed a spider
capturing a fly in its web in the imperial garden, and was struck by
the manner in which the spider maintained a strong rooted grip on
the web while it spun the fly in its silk. There were many schools of
unarmed combat at the time, several of which practiced aiki jujutsu, a
broad method of self-defense against every conceivable form of
attack, in which the attacker's strength was somehow used to aid in
his defeat.

The *aiki jujutsu* of Prince Sadazumi evolved over the generations
until the twelfth century, when it came under the leadership of
Shinra Minamoto Saburo, who was an outstanding general and man
of great medical knowledge. One of the characteristic engagements,
practiced in a myriad of ways in aikido, is defense against grabs to
the wrist and arms. This array of techniques is said to have been
emphasized by Yoshimitsu Sensei because he realized that though a
samurai enemy might wear armor, he rarely covered his hands and
wrists in order to more sensitively wield his sword. They were prime

targets because even a slight twist of a wrist or push on an elbow could unbalance an attacker.

It is said that Yoshimitsu added many applications of escape and defense against grabbing, because grabbing a warrior's hand, elbow, or arm while he was in the process of drawing his weapon slowed him and provided an opportunity to counterattack. To this day *aikidoka* practice dozens and dozens of techniques which relate to freeing the sword hand from an attack by grabbing.

Yoshimitsu's son Yoshikiyo added "sword-taking" techniques to assist an unarmed warrior against a long or short sword. It was at this time that Minamoto Yoshimitsu took the name of the town in which he lived, Takeda, which was then passed on from generation to generation. In 1868, the thirty-second in the line of Takedas, Takeda Sokaku, decided to revitalize his ancient family art and opened a dojo in Hokkaido, which he named after his estate, Daito. Here, Daito-ryu *aiki jujutsu* was born. Later, Takeda Sokaku's son, Tokimune Takeda, took over his father's dojo in the province of Abashiri, which he named Daitokan, a name it bears to this day.

Ueshiba Morihei, known as "O-sensei" (Great Teacher) and regarded as the founder of aikido, was at the time leading a band of homesteaders in Hokkaido. He came to classes taught by Takeda Sokaku at the Daitokan. Ueshiba Sensei brought with him an impressive array of martial arts specialties. As a high-ranking exponent of sword, staff, spear, and *jujutsu* before he encountered Takeda Sensei, he quickly became one of Takeda's outstanding students. Ueshiba Sensei expanded the curriculum of the Daitokan. He was twenty-eight years old at the time.

Ueshiba Sensei's dedication to his Daito-ryu teacher is legendary. He waited on his teacher day and night, cooked his meals, drew his bath, massaged his sore muscles, and even built a new home for him. Still, Takeda Sensei charged Ueshiba between ¥300 and ¥500 for each technique he taught him. In 1916, at the age of thirty-three, Ueshiba received a diploma asserting that he was a master of Daito-ryu.

An insight into aikido, the art that Ueshiba Sensei was on the verge of inventing at the time, stems from a comment he once made about living with Takeda. Takeda Sensei had trouble sleeping because of nightmares about the many men he had killed. O-Sensei said that this was one of the early experiences that convinced him that a mind of *aiki*—a truly peaceful, hence strong, mind—is filled with love, not hate and fear.

Two years later, Ueshiba left behind the village he had established and his Daito-ryu master to visit his father's sickbed. On his trip he heard about a religious leader named Deguchi Onisaburo, head of a new Shinto sect called Omotokyo, who lived in Ayabe, in Kyoto. He made a brief stop to visit Deguchi and was so impressed that after his father's funeral he returned to Ayabe.

He came back a changed man. At his father's grave, stirred powerfully by the emotion of the moment, Ueshiba vowed that he would devote himself to a lifelong quest to understand the true nature of being and the secrets of budo. Until he was forty-one, Ueshiba lived in isolation, fasting, praying, meditating, and practicing martial arts on a sacred mountain outside Ayabe.

This was a period of intense creativity for Ueshiba Sensei. His great talent for the martial arts, his many years of experience and hardship, and a religious sensitivity that had been stimulated by ancient Shinto beliefs, Zen Buddhist monks, and the founder of Omotokyo all primed him for his great experience.

In 1934 Master Ueshiba accompanied Deguchi into China, ostensibly to attempt to stop the Sino-Japanese war and to create a Kingdom of Peace. This was probably a thinly disguised espionage mission on behalf of the Japanese government. Its somewhat less than "holy" intent is seen in the fact that Chang Tso-lin, the warlord of Mukden, created an "Independent Army of the Northwest," placed it under the command of General Lu Chan-kin and put the general under the direction of Reverend Deguchi. During this time Ueshiba had many opportunities to hone his martial arts in battle and in contests with practitioners of various Chinese arts, including Mongolian wrestling.

During Ueshiba's return trip to Ayabe after his experiences in China and Manchuria, he was accosted on a desolate stretch of road by a bandit armed with a pistol. He discovered that he could see the bullets fly toward him and therefore had enough time to dodge them.

When later asked about this experience he noted that there seemed to be a very long time between the point when the bandit thought to pull the trigger and the moment he actually did it. This experience of moving at an accelerated speed, or conversely of experiencing things around you in what appears to be slow motion, is very commonly reported by great martial arts masters and talented athletes. Remember Asakuma Sensei's comment that it took a long time for the arrow to hit the target. Famous professional football player Joe Namath once said that on his best days the rush of the defensive linemen toward him seemed to come in slow motion. The "dodging bullets" story is also sometimes set in China. As with all origin stories in Japanese budo, there are many variations of the basic tale.

One spring day in 1925 when Ueshiba was forty-two he had a wonderful and life-altering experience. As he sat under a persimmon tree he was suddenly overcome by a feeling of intense heat. He perspired freely and found that he could not move. He wrote (quoted in Random, 1977: 208-09):

> I had the sensation that the universe was suddenly shaking and
> that a gold-colored spiritual energy, rising from the ground,
> shrouded my body in a veil, turning it gold. At the same time, my
> body and spirit became luminous. I could understand the chattering
> of birds and I had a clear comprehension of the intentions of God,
> the creator of the universe. At that moment, I was enlightened. I
> understood that the source of budo is love of God, the spirit of lov-
> ing protection of all creatures. Endless tears of joy ran down my
> cheeks. Since then I have realized that the whole earth is my home,
> that the sun, moon and stars are all mine. I was freed of all desire,
> not only for my position, fame or prosperity, but also for strength.
> I understood that budo does not consist of bringing down the
> enemy by force, nor is it a means of destroying the world with
> weapons: the pure spirit of budo means accepting the spirit of the
> universe, spreading peace throughout the world, speaking correctly,
> protecting and honoring all nature's creatures. I understood that the
> purpose of budo is to accept the love of God in its true sense which
> protects and cultivates all living things and that it is advisable to

use and assimilate it with our mind and body. The way of budo is to make the heart of the universe one's own heart.

In 1927 Ueshiba left Ayabe and moved with his wife and children to Tokyo, where he gathered thirty or forty students and opened a dojo he called the Kobukan. It was during this time that, realizing that *aiki jujutsu* did not adequately express his religious, philosophical, and martial experience, he changed the name of what he taught to aikido to stress that the goal of training was not to learn to kill more effectively but to serve the force of life and peace more effectively.

Master Ueshiba moved in 1938 to Iwama, about ninety-three miles north of Tokyo, where he built a dojo and a Shinto shrine and settled in to establish the art of aikido. Many of Japan's top martial artists went to Iwama to see O-Sensei and experience his art. Professor Kano Jigoro, judo's illustrious founder, observed O-Sensei, and upon his return to the Kodokan dispatched several of his students to study with Ueshiba. One of them, Tomiki Shihan, later created a style of aikido (Tomiki-ryu) which combined the aikido of Ueshiba with many of the educational and organizational features created by his judo teacher, Professor Kano.

In 1948 the growing popularity of aikido led to the creation of the Tokyo Aikikai. On April 26, 1969, Ueshiba Shihan died in Tokyo at the age of eighty-six. In his later years his philosophical and spiritual pronouncements, offered as a running commentary to his technical martial instruction, grew so esoteric that many of his students of the time report that they rarely understood them. He would say things like (Random, 1977: 211): "Aikido is not that which is expressed in movements, but what comes well before the form is born, for aikido is a part of the physical world of the Void." Practice that!

A sampling of his *Poems of the Path* clearly shows O-Sensei's desire to communicate his experiences to his students (Ueshiba, 1991: 28-29):

Rely on the majesty of the lord
who rules our world, and
advance bravely.
 O gods of heaven and earth!
We beseech you to guide us toward the

precious techniques of ki
that calm the soul and purify
all things.

The penetrating brilliance of a sword
wielded by a man of the Way
strikes at the evil enemy lurking deep
within one's own body and soul.
Ceaselessly polish the Sacred Sword
and bring forth its divinity;
a holy warrior serves the gods.

Deep and mysterious the grand design
of the Path of the Sword—
place its heat and light in your heart.
True Budo cannot be described by words or letters;
the gods will not allow you to make
such explanations.
Forge the spirit according to the divine will;
seek the light and heat of the Universal Sword
and attain enlightenment.

Aikido, with its characteristic joint-stressing techniques and many aerial throws and break-falls, is not suitable for the very young or very old, where lack of joint integration in the first case, and bone brittleness and loss in the second, can result in unsafe practice conditions. However, as is true with almost all the major marital arts in Japan, a little inquiry can often locate a children's aikido club, for example, where well-trained instructors teach the art within the physical limitations of prepubescent children.

Seniors can also practice aikido in a modified manner. For example, most aikido practitioners past their mid-fifties rarely take the many break-falls, aerial throws, and tumbling escapes that are practiced in a typical aikido class. The more fragile (due to age or illness) aikido students can practice the setup to throws and pins, then stop right before the moment of impact or body stress, and still achieve artistic and physical benefits.

Aikido is a relatively safe martial art to practice. In over twenty-five years of practice I have only seen two accidents requiring a physician's care; in both cases they were dislocated shoulders. One occurred during testing when a student took a fall incorrectly. In the other instance I dislocated my student's shoulder while demonstrating a technique during class. It surprised both of us because it was a very basic technique, one that I had done hundreds of times, and I was moving relatively slowly in order to allow the students to observe the movement required in the technique. Suddenly, I felt my partner's body stiffen as I executed the throw. His face turned gray and when he stood up his right shoulder was hanging several inches below the line of his left. We both presented quite a spectacle as we energetically apologized to each other for the accident. He assured me it was his fault for resisting my technique while I insisted that as an aikido sensei I should be in better control of my techniques. I am always upset when students are injured during my classes and I am sure that most martial arts sensei share the same feeling. Yet we practice a martial art. Pain and injury generally hover dangerously close when the "martial" is being practiced as art.

Aikido is an excellent self-defense art, based more on knowledge than brute physical strength; therefore, one cannot understand its combat effectiveness simply by watching a typical aikido class. One definition of aikido I encountered years ago was "the art of leading the mind through pain." Many who observe the "training forms" of aikido, with their large and flowing movements, mistake them for aikido's answer to techniques that might be used for self-defense "in the street." The *kihon waza*, the basic techniques of aikido, train the strength, energy, and knowledge needed for advanced students to effectively apply self-defense techniques—hard or soft, large or small, fast or slow—in harmony with the situation.

Don't mistake training forms and basics to be about "street application" except in an indirect manner. The deep training stances of Shotokan karatedo, for example, are not typical of stances spontaneously arrayed in *kumite* (sparring) conditions. Their function is to build the muscles and nerve connections that will energize the legs, hips, knees, and ankles in freestyle engagements, whether real or formal competitions, when the practitioner is most likely to be in a more natural stance.

I was made aware of the difference between training forms and real life while visiting Chan Poi Sifu, grand master of the Wah Lum Praying Mantis style of kung fu. One afternoon we were watching some of his students practice one of the more rudimentary spear forms of his style. The red tassels on the spears hissed as the students spun, jumped, flipped, parried, and stabbed in unison. Chan Sifu turned to me and said, "Some people call my kung fu 'dancing.' They see the open view but not the hidden view." He took a spear from the weapons' rack. "That," he said pointing to his students, "is an exercise form. I will show you the hidden form, the fighting form." It is always an astounding experience to watch a true martial arts master up close. He performed the ritualized opening movements to the fighting form and began. I could recognize the basic structure of the spear form since I had been watching the kung fu students repeat this form for about an hour. Chan Sifu crouched and lunged, his spear blade flashing. But his form was simpler and more focused on stabbing with great power. It looked like a long-staff *kata* in karate. It was clear that the training or exercise form was the mechanism that built the students' strength and skill to be able to accomplish some very basic things with maximum power—the block, parry, and strike which were the heart and soul of the fighting form the Sifu demonstrated.

Always assume that you don't know what's happening behind the exercise form you are requested to master as a budo student. You couldn't possibly know. This kind of knowledge is "body knowledge." A teacher can show you how to do an advanced maneuver, but the student cannot "know" how to do the same maneuver until the right moment, a moment of which a budo teacher is acutely aware.

The vastness of budo training was suggested when an interviewer asked Ueshiba Morihei what aikido was. The master's response was: "a sleeping giant." All the budo arts are sleeping giants. It is always best to remain humble, to take one step at a time. As you practice budo you are scratching the surface of an enormous presence. An awareness that should drive the student of the martial arts onward is the growing knowledge, gleaned through long practice, that there is much, much more just down the road a little, just behind that last row of trees, if you only keep on going.

The world center of aikido is the Aikikai Hombu Dojo located at 17-18 Wakamatsu-cho, Shinjuku, Tokyo 162.-0056. Tel: (03) 3203-9236 or (03) 3204-8145. Fax: (03) 3204-8145. Or log on to the Web site at www.aikikai.org. The Hombu is a five-story building constructed in 1968 with three major training areas and a total training area of 250 mats. Direct your inquiries to the International Department under the directorship of Mr. Yonemochi.

You are welcome to observe classes at the Aikikai Hombu Dojo or sample practice for about ¥2000 mat fee. Training begins at 6:30 a.m. and ends after the evening class from 7:00–8:00 p.m., each class period being about an hour. The sessions are organized into three broad categories: general training, beginners' classes, and women's classes. There are also special training categories, organized from time to time, for dancers, policemen, children, and weapons specialists (sword, staff, knife).

The quality of aikido instructors at the Aikikai Hombu Dojo is, of course, exceptional. For example, if you were to practice at the 8:00 a.m. class on Monday, you would receive instruction from Seki Shoji Shihan (seventh-degree black belt), and if you were a member of the beginners' class practicing on Monday evening, your teacher would be Miyamoto Tsuruzo Shihan (seventh- degree black belt). In fact, most of the Hombu instructors are ranked as sixth- to eighth-degree black belts!

The Hombu's rules of etiquette are as follows (from www.aiki-web.com/misc/etiquette.html):

1. When entering or leaving the dojo, it is proper to bow in the direction of O-Sensei's picture, the kamiza, or the front of the dojo. You should also bow when entering or leaving the mat.
2. No shoes on mat.
3. Be on time for class. Students should be lined up and seated in seiza approximately 3-5 minutes before the official start of class. If you do happen to arrive late, sit quietly in seiza on the edge of the mat until the instructor grants permission to join practice.
4. If you should leave the mat or dojo for any reason during class, approach the instructor and ask permission.

5. Avoid sitting on the mat with your back to the picture of O-Sensei. Also, do not lean against the walls or sit with your legs stretched out. (Either sit in seiza or cross-legged.)

6. Remove watches, rings and other jewelry before practice as they may catch a partner's hair, skin, or clothing and cause injury to oneself or one's partner.

7. Do not bring food, gum, or beverages onto the mat. It is also considered disrespectful in traditional dojo to bring open food or beverages into the dojo.

8. Please keep your fingernails (and especially one's toenails) clean and cut short.

9. Please keep talking during class to a minimum. What conversation there is should be restricted to one topic—aikido. It is particularly impolite to talk while the instructor is addressing the class.

10. If you are having trouble with a technique, do not shout across the room to the instructor for help. First, try to figure the technique out by watching others. Effective observation is a skill you should strive to develop as well as any other in your training. If you still have trouble, approach the instructor at a convenient moment and ask for help.

11. Carry out the directives of the instructor promptly. Do not keep the rest of the class waiting for you.

12. Do not engage in rough-housing or needless contests of strength during class.

13. Keep your training uniform clean, in good shape, and free of offensive odor.

14. Please pay your membership dues promptly. If, for any reason, you are unable to pay your dues on time, talk with the person in charge of dues collection. Sometimes special rates are available for those experiencing financial hardship.

15. Change your clothes only in designated areas (not on the mat!).

16. Remember you are in a class to learn, and not to gratify your ego. An attitude of receptivity and humility (though not obsequiousness) is therefore advised.

17. It is usually considered polite to bow upon receiving assistance or correction from the instructor.

18. During class, if the instructor is assisting a group in your vicinity, it is frequently considered appropriate to suspend your own training so that the instructor has adequate room to demonstrate.

The dojo regulations prescribed by O-Sensei himself are of a more subtle nature than most "rules of the dojo" you will find posted in all martial arts' dojo (from www.aikiweb.com/general/dojo-reg.html):

1. Aikido decides life and death in a single strike, so students must carefully follow the instructor's teaching and not compete to see who is the strongest.
2. Aikido is the Way that teaches how one can deal with several enemies. Students must train themselves to be alert not just to the front but to all sides and the back.
3. Training should always be conducted in a pleasant and joyful atmosphere.
4. The instructor teaches only one small aspect of the art. Its versatile applications must be discovered by each student through incessant practice and training.
5. In daily practice first begin by moving your body and then progress to more intensive practice. Never force anything unnaturally or unreasonably. If this rule is followed, then even elderly people will not hurt themselves and they can train in a pleasant and joyful atmosphere.
6. The purpose of aikido is to train mind and body and to produce sincere, earnest people. Since all the techniques are to be transmitted person-to-person, do not randomly reveal them to others, for this might lead to their being used by hoodlums.

As in other Japanese martial arts, there are a number of aikido styles. I saw only Hombu aikido, or Ueshiba-ryu aikido, during my travels in Japan, and it always seemed to go without saying that unless otherwise stated the aikido being practiced was that of the *shihan* teaching at the Hombu Dojo in Tokyo.

The three other styles of aikido that one might encounter in Japan, and elsewhere, are Yoshinkan , Tomiki-ryu, and Shinshin Toitsu aikido. These (and others) are sometimes called "breakaway schools." In most cases the separation from the current Hombu style came about quite naturally. O-Sensei's aikido evolved throughout his life. When one of O-Sensei's senior students would, due to family responsibilities or occupational needs, leave the master's dojo and establish his own aikido class wherever his responsibilities took him, he would naturally teach the aikido that O-Sensei had been teaching at the time. Once in relative isolation from O-Sensei, the senior student, now a sensei in his own right, would tend to execute techniques in a manner most suitable to his own body, age, and personality. Meanwhile, O-Sensei's aikido kept growing and changing. At a later date, if one were to compare the aikido of the "breakaway" schools with the Hombu Aikido, some differences could be seen. Sometimes these differences were of a major proportion. Tomiki Sensei's addition of competitive fighting in his style of aikido (inspired by judo) is an example of a very large difference, while in most cases the differences are a matter of foot positioning or *kamae* (fighting attitude) or small technical aspects of a basic technique.

The Yoshinkan aikido style was developed by Kancho Shioda Gozo Kancho (1914–94). Shioda Sensei became a disciple of Ueshiba Morihei at the age of eighteen and spent the next eight years of his life as a full-time student of aikido. In the first martial arts exposition sanctioned in Japan after World War II, Shioda Sensei's exhibition of aikido drew the interest of a number of businessmen and politicians who encouraged him to open the Yoshinkan Aikidojo. This became the center of the worldwide spread of Shioda Shihan's aikido. Shioda Shihan had the following to say about aikido:

> As you grow older, your muscles weaken, and you can't lift or pull as when you were young. This kind of power is limited and it cannot help but decline no matter how much you try to build it. So, as Ueshiba Sensei said, the key to unlimited strength is kokyu ryoku, "breath power." It is, in fact, based on natural principles. When your opponent tries to use his power against you, you can simply absorb it into your own. Therefore, you don't need to use force yourself.
>
> Aikido is said to be the martial art of wa (harmony). It is not difficult to explain this. When you see your opponent, you possess both a personality and power which make your opponent feel that

he doesn't want to fight with you. This becomes *wa*. It does not mean that you compromise. *Wa* is only possible when you have "something strong" within yourself that makes your opponent your friend, and makes them cooperate with you. This is called *tai sureba ai wasu* which means that when you see your opponent, you harmonize. This is only possible when you have *toku*, "virtue," the foundation of which lies in your *chushin ryoku*, "center power."

To inquire about training in Yoshinkan aikido while in Japan, contact:

Ando Tsuneo Shihan, 4-19-1-101 Tomioka, Urayasu-shi, Chiba-ken, 279-0021 Japan. Tel and fax: (047) 353-7140.

Tomiki-ryu aikido is the creation of one of Kano Jigoro Shihan's senior students, Tomiki Kenji. Tomiki Sensei was interested in "rationalizing" aikido practice. Master Ueshiba, lacking formal education, developed aikido out of his own insight and enlightenment. Tomiki Sensei, following his teacher Kano Sensei, sought to develop an aikido style that could be fit, like judo, into modern concepts of education. One of his major departures from the teaching of Ueshiba Sensei had to do with the role, if any, of competitions in aikido. Ueshiba Sensei was strongly opposed to competition, feeling that it had no place in his vision of aikido. Tomiki Sensei, on the other hand, influenced by his teacher, Professor Kano, thought that competitions would serve to sharpen the concentration and focus of his students. In Tomiki-ryu aikido, competitions are based on performance of *kata* (prearranged forms) and freestyle reactions against empty-handed attacks and attacks with a *tanto*, or knife (usually made of rubber for the sake of safe practice).

Tomiki Sensei was a very accomplished man in his own right. He was a national judo champion in Japan, rising ultimately to the level of eighth-degree black belt. He also achieved a ninth-degree black belt in aikido, as well as gaining a Ph.D. in economics. In 1954, while working as an economics professor at prestigious Waseda University in Tokyo, Tomiki Sensei headed the university's physical education department. In 1958 he founded the Waseda University Aikido Club and in 1967 opened the Shodokan Dojo for the study of aikido. Seven years later he founded the Japan Aikido Federation, and in 1975 he was elected vice president of the Nippon Budo Gakkai (the Martial Art Society of Japan). A year later, he established the Shodokan Headquarters in Osaka for the study of aikido. Tomiki Kenji Shihan passed away on December 25, 1979 at the age of seventy-nine.

The name Shodokan was selected by Tomiki Sensei to honor the Showa period (*sho*) in which the Shodokan was founded and to acknowledge Kano Sensei's dojo (*do*), while *kan* suggests a facility that houses an organization or group. Today the Shodokan is the center of the Japan Aikido Association and Tomiki-ryu aikido, sometimes called Shodokan aikido.

To inquire about practicing Tomiki-ryu aikido while in Japan, contact:

Nariyama Tetsuro
Shodokan International Headquarters
1-28-7 Hannan-cho, Abeno-ku, Osaka-shi
Osaka-fu 545-0021, Japan

If it might be said that Ueshiba Morihei was powerfully influenced by mystical Shintoism and Tomiki Sensei by the rational and competitive "sports" concepts of the founder of judo, Tohei Koichi Shihan was strongly influenced by Zen meditation, a practice he began as a young boy at the urging of his father. Tohei Sensei's fateful meeting with Ueshiba took place in 1939 when he was nineteen years old, but his serious practice of aikido under O-Sensei did not begin until after World War II, when he became one of the *uchi deshi* (inner students) of O-Sensei, living with the master and training daily in aikido. In 1953 O-Sensei sent Tohei Sensei to open an *aikidojo* in Hawaii, making him the first to introduce aikido to the United States.

Later, Tohei Shihan rose to the position of chief instructor at the Aikikai Hombu Dojo and was the only *aikidoka* awarded the rank of tenth-degree black belt by O-Sensei. In 1971 Tohei Sensei, while still acting as chief instructor at the Hombu, founded the Ki no Kenkyukai (Ki Society International) to focus on teaching methods of *ki* meditation. After resigning as Hombu chief instructor he founded the Shinshin Toitsu Aikikai.

To sample the thinking of Tohei Shihan on the meaning of aikido I will quote from a talk he gave to the Ki no Kenkyukai (from http//:omlc.ogi.edu/aikido/talk/tohei/shokushu/):

"Let us have a universal spirit that loves and protects all creation and helps all things grow and develop. To unify mind and body and become one with the Universe is the ultimate purpose of my study. Our lives are born of the *ki* of the Universe. Let us give thanks for being born not as plants and animals, but as lords of creation. Let us pledge to fulfill our missions by helping to guide the development and creation of the Universe. The absolute Universe is one. We call this *ki*. Our life and body are born of the *ki* of the Universe. We study thoroughly the principles of the Universe and practice them. We are one with the Universe. There is no need to despond, no need to fear. The way we follow is the Way of the Universe, which no difficulty nor hardship can hinder. Let us have the courage to say with Confucius, 'If I have a clear conscience and a calm spirit, I dare to face an enemy of ten thousand men.' Do not think that the power you have is only the power you ordinarily use and moan that you have little strength. The power you ordinarily use is like the small, visible segment of an iceberg. The Universe is a limitless circle with a limitless radius. This condensed becomes the One Point in the lower abdomen which is the center of the Universe. Let us concentrate our mind in this One Point and become one with and send our *ki* constantly to the Universe. Like the calm, still surface of the water that reflects the moon and a flying bird, true living calmness is the condition of our mind that reflects all things clearly. This is man's original and natural state."

To learn about where you can practice Shinshin Toitsu aikido, please contact:

International Director
Shinshin Toitsu Aikido Shoshinkan
1-12-25 Ninomiya, Tsukuba-shi, Ibaraki-ken 305-0051, Japan

If you are interested in the *ki* training and meditative aspects of Shinshin Toitsu Aikido, write to either of the following:
Ki Society World Headquarters (Ki no Kenkyukai Sohombu)
3515 Oaza Akabane, Ichikai-machi, Haga-gun
Tochigi-ken 321-3426, Japan. Tel: (0285) 68-4000

Ki Society Tokyo Headquarters (Ki No Kenkyukai Tokyo)
101 Ushigome Heim, 2-30 Haramachi, Shinjuku-ku
Tokyo 162-0053, Japan

Before leaving the discussion of aikido it is necessary to touch upon the practice of one of the technical roots of modern aikido, Daito-ryu *aiki jujutsu*. In discussing the historical sources of modern aikido I outlined the story of the great Takeda Sokaku (1859–1943) and his Daito-ryu. Whereas Ueshiba Morihei, acting under his own spiritual insight, creative genius, and high rank in swordsmanship, spear fighting, and various forms of *jujutsu*, modeled his art into what he would come to call aikido (as opposed to *aiki jujutsu*), the Takeda line continued to teach the original Daito-ryu *aiki jujutsu*.

For information about the practice of Daito-ryu *aiki jujutsu*, you may contact:

Daito-ryu Jujutsu Headquarters
(Daito-ryu Aiki Jujutsu Hombu)
2-10-15 Higashi Yotsugi, Katsushika-ku, Tokyo 124-0014, Japan

For e-mail contact with the Daito-ryu headquarters in English: dsteel@daito-ryu.org.

Naginatado: The Way of the Naginata

The naginata is based on the Chinese kwanto, a bronze halberd, or bladed-staff weapon. In its Japanese form it is a staff about two to three yards in length to which is attached a slightly curved metal blade that can be from twelve to twenty-four inches long and as sharp as a sword. The practice of the naginata-wielding art must stand as one of Japan's oldest martial arts, maybe even older than the formal study of swordsmanship, though not the bow.

The length of the naginata enabled those fighting on foot to hamstring the horses of the enemy with the bladed end, and then keep the unseated samurai at bay with the superior length of the weapon. This weapon also enabled the *naginatadoka* to attack the legs of a swordsman at a distance and to keep him on the defensive. The swordsman's only tactic was to find some lapse in the naginata fighter's defense and rush him before he could bring the long weapon to bear. Many samurai lost their legs to this weapon.

The oldest naginata school dates to A.D. 1168 Its worth in battle was first documented in a battle at Dannoura in A.D. 1185, which set the Taira clan against the Minamoto. By the Muromachi era (1336–1574) there were 425 naginata *ryu* in Japan. The naginata lost its position as a valued samurai weapon in the late sixteenth century with the introduction of firearms into Japanese warfare.

After the Onin War (1467–77) when the *yari* (spear), a lighter, shorter, and more maneuverable weapon than the naginata, grew in popularity, the naginata began to fade from common use by the samurai but was maintained by some monastic orders for exercise and self-defense and by women of the samurai class, for whom it was seen as a home-defense weapon. After the 1600s, the naginata became mainly associated with women, and is still taught in many girls' colleges and schools. In almost all cases it is exclusive to women. Naginatado teaches posture, elegance of movement, stamina, and focus while serving as an excellent exercise form. This art and *sado* (the tea ceremony) remain common components in the modern education of "proper" Japanese young women. The Japanese men who become interested in naginatado today are generally those with a long history of experience in swordsmanship. It is estimated that there are about 500,000 women practitioners of naginatado worldwide.

Naginatado, besides the constant practice of *kihon waza* (basic techniques), also features sparring and sports competition in its repertoire. The naginata used in sparring is a little under seven feet in length, with a blade constructed along the lines of the *shinai* of kendo. When sparring, *naginatadoka* wear kendo armor with the addition of the *suneate* (shin guard), the shins being a viable target in naginata fighting but not in kendo.

Women *naginatadoka* have played prominent parts in Japan's long martial history. Over a thousand years ago Japanese Empress Jingo, though pregnant at the time, led her troops against the Korean kingdom of Silla. Her weapons were the sword, bow, and naginata. When the Silla defenders saw the Empress and her army approach, they fled. The Empress had her naginata mounted over the gate to the Silla castle as a memorial to her victory.

Many famous Japanese heroines wielded the naginata. Tomoe Gozen, medieval Japanese woman warrior, used a naginata to defeat a dozen sword-wielding attackers who attempted to take a bridge that she was ordered to defend. In the twelfth century General Minamoto Yoritomo was saved from death by a Zen nun named Ike Gozen who came to his defense with a naginata, and in 1185 the young Emperor Antoku was saved from assassination by the mistress of Tomotori, who repelled the assassins with her naginata. In 1189, Fujinoe defended Takadachi Castle and in public combat on the palace stairs she defeated two prominent swordsmen, Yamato Juro and Nagasawa Uemon Taro using her naginata.

To inquire about naginata training while in Japan, contact:

International Naginata Federation
3-2-9 Nishidai Itami-shi
Hyogo-ken 664-0858, Japan
Tel: (0727) 75-2838
Fax: (0727) 72-2062

Jodo: The Way of the Staff

Practicing the jo (short staff) in my years of aikido and studying its history and styles led me to inquire about Shinto Muso-ryu jodo when I moved to Fukuoka, one of the centers of jodo. I began my practice of jodo at the Fukuoka Budokan and was taken on a trip to Dazaifu, a sacred site on the island of Kyushu, where the remains of Master Muso Gonnosuke Katsuyoshi are interred at a Shinto shrine. On this trip, my sensei related the following story of the origins of Muso-ryu jodo. A number of variations on this story are found in both the oral tradition and in the pertinent literature. The historical accounts of the engagements between Miyamoto Musashi and Muso Gonnosuke that led to the founding of Shinto Muso-ryu jodo are found in the Kaijo Monogatari, written in 1629, and in the Honcho Bugei Koden, compiled in 1714. Some versions depict Muso as a bully and braggart who badgered Musashi into a match, while others depict Muso as the compliant one and Musashi as the lout.

In the early seventeenth century Miyamoto Musashi, the "Sword Saint," wandered Japan challenging masters of various martial styles to test his sword skills. When he arrived on the island of Kyushu he was told of a famous bo (long staff) and sword master and Shinto priest named Muso Gonnosuke Katsuyoshi of the Katori Shinto-ryu and he set out to find him to issue a challenge. The match was arranged. It was to be a practice match using wooden weapons, which really did not minimize the danger. Remember that Musashi killed the second greatest swordsman in Japan with a wooden sword.

Master Muso confidently faced the great Musashi with a six-foot staff (*bo*) in June 1605. Some accounts describe Muso's weapon as a very large (four-foot-long) *bokken*. The fight progressed furiously, with neither man able to prevail. Finally, Musashi stepped back from Muso and said, "You are a great warrior, and I don't wish to harm you." Master Muso, however, was humiliated. Musashi had "allowed" him to live. This was an insult to a samurai, but Muso secretly knew that Musashi was right. If the fight had continued, Muso would have been defeated. But how could that be? The *bo* was longer than Musashi's wooden sword. And, whereas Master Muso could strike with both ends of his weapon, Musashi could attack only with one end. Further, Musashi's sword had only one edge, whereas all surfaces of a staff weapon are its edge. Muso could not understand how he could have lost to Musashi with all the advantages the long staff offered against a swordfighter. In a deep quandary Muso Gonnosuke Katsuyoshi retired to a mountain cottage in the hills surrounding Daizaifu to contemplate his duel with Musashi.

After thirty-seven days of meditation and contemplation, Master Muso had a dream. A young boy, or spirit, came to Muso in the night and showed him three weapons that seemed to dance in the air before his eyes. The boy/spirit then disappeared, and Muso saw that the three weapons that hovered tremulously in the air before him were a *katana* (sword), a *yari* (spear), and a naginata (halberd). Suddenly the three weapons collapsed into one and a *jo* (short staff) appeared. He was enlightened to the fact that the *jo* could be wielded as a spear, a sword, and a naginata. He saw in the one-inch-thick polished staff, reaching from the ground to the level of the heart, that he actually had three weapons in one! He could reap and slash like a *naginatadoka*, cut and block like a swordsman, and jab and parry like a spear fighter.

The child/spirit said only one thing to Master Muso: "Strike *suigetsu!*" The Japanese term means "moon in the water," or more prosaically, the diaphragm. This is a prime target of the *jodoka* because a swordsman must raise his arms in order to strike, thus exposing his diaphragm for a fraction of a second. A sharp strike to this area can kill or seriously incapacitate an opponent.

Muso practiced with his new weapon until he felt he was ready to challenge Musashi to a rematch. In the second encounter, after a minute of furious engagement, Musashi jumped back from Master Muso and pulled open his jacket to reveal a one-inch-diameter bruise above his heart. Muso had delivered a killing blow in a *yari* jab to the heart but had aimed it a few inches high to honor the spirit of the match. But Musashi had lost! This was the only time in his entire history that he was defeated in match contests. Later, Muso and Musashi were hired as weapons teachers by Lord Kuroda of Kumamoto in central Kyushu and they both retired in the service of this great *daimyo* (feudal lord).

Shinto Muso-ryu jodo begins with basic *jo* training (strikes, blocks, parries, jabs) and progresses to twelve *kata* which feature an encounter between a swordsman armed with a *bokken* and a *jo* fighter, a ritual nod to the classic confrontation between Musashi and Muso. The completion of these *kata* forms the basis of ranking to the level of first-degree black belt. After this point, the training includes use of the *jo* against the *wakazashi* (short sword), and later a novel form of *kusari* (weighted chain). Contests in Muso-ryu do not involve freestyle sparring matches between *jo* and bokken, but rather *kata* competition.

Shinto Muso-ryu jodo presently is taught to special units of the Japanese police. For example, the policemen who patrolled the grounds of the American consulate in Fukuoka were armed with *jo*. The art seems to be mainly centered in Fukuoka, Tokyo, the Osaka-Kyoto area, Kanagawa, and Aichi prefecture.

To inquire concerning access to a Shinto Muso-ryu *jodojo*, you may contact:

Zen Nippon Kendo Renmei, Jodo Division
c/o Nippon Budokan
2-3 Kitanomaru Koen
Chiyoda-ku, Tokyo 102-0091, Japan

Iaido: The Way of Drawing the Sword

The *ai* of *iaido* suggests a harmonious or adaptable or appropriate component, whereas the *i* points to the coexistence of body and spirit (body and spirit as one). The *do* indicates that the intent of the art is to positively affect one's way of life. The term *iaido* is derived from the Japanese phrase *tsune ni ite, kyu ni awasu*, which means something like, "Whatever you are doing and wherever you may be, be prepared for any eventuality."

Historically, the art of the sword was divided into roughly two categories, *iaijutsu* and *kenjutsu*. The latter involved the use of the sword outside the scabbard. *Iaijutsu* focused on the techniques of drawing the blade, utilizing it, and returning it to the scabbard. The basics of sword drawing of the *iaijutsu* schools involved *nukitsuke*, the drawing of the sword; *kiritsuke*, killing with one stroke; *chiburi*, flicking blood from the sword's blade, and *noto*, returning the sword to its scabbard.

One of the earliest schools of fast draw with sword was the Tenshin Shoden Katori Shinto-ryu which was developed about 1460 by Iizasa Choisai. Modern iaido, as opposed to *iaijutsu*, was pioneered by Hayashizaki Jinsuke, who in the sixteenth century emphasized the methods of drawing the sword more for self-training than for warfare.

In that differentiation, the germ of the idea of modern iaido can be seen. Master Hayashizaki traveled throughout Japan teaching his ideas about the use of the sword as a method of self-cultivation and was responsible for the opening of about two hundred schools devoted to his ideas and methods. By the time of the seventeenth grand master in this line, the art of drawing the sword was divided between two schools, the Muso Jikiden Eishin-ryu centered in Kanagawa, and the Muso Shinden-ryu, which is more prevalent in the Tokyo area.

The intent of the modern advocates of Iaido is to utilize the intense concentration required to master the basic *kata* of their style as a form of meditation and self-discipline. Its outer form is one of grandeur, solitude, mental and spiritual focus, and martial intent. It is an art of simple but chilling beauty and austerity. The only physical requirement is the ability to move from sitting to kneeling to standing and back again, usually in slow motion. The wielding of the *iaito*, the swords designed for iaido practice, offers exercise to the wrists and arms. Light exercise though it may be, the mental requirements are such that this "light" exercise can be exhausting, if satisfyingly so.

Needed for practice, besides an *iaito* and *saya* (scabbard), are a *dogi* and *hakama*. Buying your practice uniform in Japan will be more expensive than purchasing one in the United States. As for the *iaito*, the one I most recently purchased, a medium-grade weapon, cost $500. As for *shinken* (real Japanese swords), the prices will range from several thousand dollars up.

In the late 1950s the All Japan Kendo Federation invited some of the greatest living exponents of iaido to form a standardized set of *kata* for training. This group created the set of *kata* that is today the basis of the All Japan Kendo Federation Basic Exercises (Zen Nihon Kendo Renmei Seitei Kata). For information concerning the location of a *iaidojo* near your residence in Japan, contact:

Dai Nippon Iaido Renmei
c/o All Japan Kendo Federation
2F Yasukuni–Kudan Minami Bldg.
2-3-14, Kudan Minami, Chiyoda-ku
Tokyo 102-0074, Japan
Tel: (03) 3234-6271. Fax: (03) 3234-6007

Ninjutsu: The Art of Stealth

The ninja are known throughout the world for their black outfits and exotic weapons. The beginnings of ninjutsu reach back to around 500 to 300 B.C. and describe specialists in espionage, or "stealth." The classic The Art of War by the Chinese general Sun Tzu features a section on methods of espionage. The term ninjutsu (methods of stealth) was used in all military arts and meant that "stealing in," "invisibility," "concealment," or "espionage" was a study in itself.

The ninja, organized in terms of family groups, did not take on the burden of "honorable" combat that restricted the samurai. When there were necessary missions that the honor-bound samurai could not or would not accept, the ninja were hired. They made infiltration of enemy headquarters a specialized art, called *tori no jutsu*. Infiltrating enemy lines during times of warfare became a ninja specialization called *chikairi no jutsu*.

Ninja employed state-of-the-art weaponry in their martial repertoires, whereas the weapons of the samurai class were often restricted to traditional weapons of the class—sword, spear, knife, and halberd. The ninja employed the samurai weapons, with their own variations, plus a variety of other items. They used shorter and straighter swords than the samurai and were famous for their lightning sword draws.

Whereas the samurai generally wore their swords on the left hip, the ninja were more likely to carry their short swords on their backs.

Blades were used in a variety of forms. Some were thrown by hand, while others were projected by hidden springs. They employed short bows instead of the classic longbow found in modern kyudo, as well as blowguns, roped hooks, garrotes, spikes, brass knuckles, dirks, darts, star-shaped throwing knives, poisoned darts, acid-spurting tubes, flash powder, smoke bombs, caltrops, and firearms.

Ninjutsu also employed *saiminjutsu* (hypnosis) and sleight of hand, as well as instruction in disguises used in "stealing in." The three most common disguises enabled the ninja to play the part of an old woman, an old man, or a Komuso monk.

Ninja could climb sheer walls utilizing special climbing equipment. They could control their breath to an incredible degree (enabling them to stay underwater for long periods). They could slow their heart rate in order to "disappear" from those searching for them. They could leap from castle walls, escape ropes and chains used to bind them, walk or run for very long distances, and remain still for hours, even days.

Ninja first appear as a deciding factor in warfare during the reign of Prince Regent Shotoku (A.D. 574–622). They were hired by the monasteries of warrior monks to augment their numbers during times of strife. During the Kamakura period (1185–1334) there were twenty-five major ninja centers, most of which were located in Iga and Koga provinces. The ninja became so powerful, in fact, that Oda Nobunaga (1534–82), one of the architects of modern Japan, employed an army of sixty-four thousand men against the Sandayu clan at Ueno and succeeded in killing four thousand ninja. The most recent classic deployment of ninja was during the Shimabara Rebellion in 1637.

To delve a little more deeply into the spirit of ninjutsu I will focus on the comments and ruminations of a few of the masters of Togakure-ryu ninjutsu. In 1891 the thirty-second grand master of this school offered these pithy comments as his New Year's message (from www.ninjutsu.com/source p.1, 1999):

1. Know the wisdom of being patient during times of inactivity.

2. Choose the course of justice as the path of your life.
3. Do not allow your heart to be controlled by the demands of desire, pleasure, or dependence.
4. Sorrow, pain, and resentment are natural qualities to be found in life; therefore, work to cultivate an immovable spirit.
5. Hold in your heart the importance of respect for your seniors, and pursue the literary and martial arts with balanced determination.

The following is derived from "The Essence of Ninjutsu" by Takamatsu Toshitsugu, the thirty-third grand master of Togakure-ryu (from www.ninjutsu.com):

> The essence of all martial art and military strategies is self-protection and the prevention of danger. Ninjutsu epitomizes the fullest concept of self-protection through martial training in that the ninja art deals with the protection of not only the physical body, but the mind and spirit as well. The way of the ninja is the way of enduring, surviving, and prevailing over all that would destroy one. Ninjutsu is the way of attaining that which we need while making the world a better place. The skill of the ninja is winning. If an expert in the fighting arts sincerely pursues the essence of ninjutsu, devoid of the influence of the ego's desires, the student will progressively come to realize the ultimate secret of becoming invincible—the attainment of the "mind and eyes of god." In tune with the providence of heaven and the impartial justice of nature, and following a clear and pure heart full of trust in the inevitable, the ninja captures the insight that will guide him successfully into battle when he must conquer and conceal himself protectively from hostility when he must acquiesce. The vast universe, beautiful in its coldly impersonal totality, contains all that we call good or bad, all the answers for all the paradoxes we see around us.

The current grand master (the thirty-fourth) of Togakure-ryu, Hatsumi Masaaki, has this to say about the heart of ninjitsu (from www.ninjutsu.com):

> I believe the ninpo, the highest order of ninjutsu, should be offered to the world as a guiding influence for all martial artists. Personal

enlightenment can only come about through total immersion in the martial tradition as a way of living. By experiencing the confrontation of danger, the transcendence of the fear of injury or death, and working knowledge of individual personal powers and limitations, the practitioner of ninjutsu can gain the strength and invincibility that permit enjoyment of the flowers moving in the wind, appreciation of the love of others, and contentment with the presence of peace in society. The attainment of this enlightenment is characterized by the development of the jihi no kokoro, or "benevolent heart." Stronger than love itself, the benevolent heart is capable of encompassing all that constitutes universal justice and all that finds expression in the unfolding of the universal scheme. Born of the insight attained from repeated exposure to the very brink between life and death, the benevolent heart of ninpo is the key to finding harmony and understanding in the realms of the spiritual and natural material worlds. Forget your sadness, grudges and hatred. Let them pass like smoke caught in a breeze. You should not deviate from the path of righteousness; you should lead a life worthy of a man. Don't be possessed by greed, luxury, or your ego. You should accept sorrows, sadness and hatred as they are, and consider them a chance for trial given to you by the powers… a blessing given by nature.

Inquire about training in Togakure-ryu ninjutsu by contacting the following sources:

Bujinkan Hombu Dojo
636 Noda, Noda-shi, Chiba-ken 278-0037, Japan

Bujinkan Dojo, Ayase Training
Tokyo Budokan
3-20-1 Ayase, Adachi-ku, Tokyo 120-0005, Japan
Tel: (03) 5697-2111

The dojo rules for practice at Bujinkan Dojo are as follows (from www.ninjutsu.com):

1. The Bujinkan shall be open to only those who agree with and uphold the guidelines of the Bujinkan Dojo. Those not doing so

shall not be allowed to join. Specifically: Only those who have read and agreed with these guidelines shall be allowed to participate.

2. Only those able to exercise true patience, self-control, and dedication shall be allowed to participate. A physician's examination report shall be required. Specifically, individuals with mental illness, drug addiction, or mental instability shall be barred from joining. The necessity of such a report concerns individuals who may present a danger to others, for example, those with infectious diseases or illnesses, individuals with clinically abnormal personalities or physiology, and individuals lacking self-control.

3. Individuals with criminal records shall be turned away. Troublemakers, those who commit crimes, and those living in Japan who break domestic laws shall be turned away.

4. Those not upholding the guidelines of the Bujinkan, either as practitioners or as members of society, by committing disgraceful or reproachable acts shall be expelled. Until now, the Bujinkan was open to large numbers of people who came to Japan. Among them, unfortunately, were those committing violent drunken acts, the mentally ill, and troublemakers who thought only of themselves and failed to see how their actions might adversely affect others. Through their actions, such people were discarding the traditional righteous heart of the Bujinkan. From this day forward, all such people shall be expelled.

5. Regarding accidents occurring during training (both inside and outside the dojo), one should not cause trouble to the Bujinkan. This is an extremely important point. Those unwilling to take personal responsibility for accidents occurring during Bujinkan training shall not be admitted. Reiterating for clarity, the Bujinkan shall not take responsibility for any accidents happening in the course of training regardless of the location.

6. All those joining the Bujinkan must get an annual member's card. This card not only preserves the honor of the Bujinkan members, it indicates you are part of a larger whole—one whose members come together with warrior hearts to better themselves through training and friendship. It evinces the glory of warrior virtue, and embodies both loyalty and brotherly love.

7. The tradition of the Bujinkan recognizes nature and the universality of all human life, and is aware of that which flows naturally between the two parts: "The secret principle of taijutsu is to know the foundations of peace." And "To study is the path to the immovable heart (fudoshin)."

My encounter with the world of the ninja came accidentally one day when a group of us went into the hills outside Fukuoka to visit a local "culture arts" center. There were dyers and woodcarvers, toymakers and calligraphy specialists. My sons were the first to spot the ninja, actually a mannequin dressed in black ninja garb that lurked along the top of a tall wooden fence that backed onto the forest which surrounded the arts center. The sign over the gate read *Ninja Mura* (Ninja Village). For a small fee one could "challenge the ninja" by entering a maze of forest paths that were festooned with ninja alarms, mainly a variety of triggers that set wood and bamboo pieces rattling and banging, ostensibly alerting the ninja in the area. There were wobbly bridges and wall-climbing obstacles. Ninja figures could be seen lying along tree branches high above the path or crouching in the shadows of dense thickets.

After hiking and climbing through the forest, one came to the "moats" that stood before the ninja house. These were real moats that could be crossed only by various rope-walking or rope-climbing techniques. A ninjutsu student waited at the water hazards to give a brief demonstration of how one uses ropes to cross moats. Of course, for the less hardy there was a path around the obstacles. Finally, one entered the ninja house, an otherwise normal-looking large Japanese farmhouse filled with a variety of secret passages and hidden sliding panels.

As we played in the Ninja Mura, I noticed that some of the obstacles looked like real training devices, especially the rope-walking and climbing obstacles over and around water hazards, while some looked like they were consciously made for children and tourists. I was later told that a real ninjutsu dojo was located on the premises and that the ninja family who owned the facilities allowed use of some of its equipment and property during the day as a way to help finance the dojo, which held its training sessions at night when the Ninja Mura was closed to the public.

The Samurai

As among flowers the cherry is queen,
so among men the samurai is lord.
—*Japanese folksong*

To varying degrees, most of the Japanese martial arts look to the samurai for their model. Some, such as ninjutsu and kobudo (the use of farm tools as weapons), however, take their inspiration from other sources: the model of espionage agents on the one hand, and Okinawan farmers on the other—both groups often enemies to the samurai class. Still, I would maintain that the general spirit of the samurai is what most Japanese martial arts are attempting to replicate most of the time, even modern ninjutsu and kobudo schools. I think that is made clear by comparing the virtues of bushido (the way of the warrior) with those presented in the previous chapter by various ninjutsu masters.

It is important that Westerners understand that the military caste of Japan has roots reaching back to the earliest days of Japanese civilization and that its code of behavior and lifestyle had a most significant impact on the shaping of modern Japanese culture. Between A.D. 300 and A.D. 500 people in the area of the present-day Kobe-Osaka-Kyoto triangle began to bury their elite dead in huge stone sarcophagi covered by keyhole-shaped earthen mounds called *kofun*, a name which came to be applied to these peoples and the era in which they flourished. The culture of the Kofun peoples blended the earlier Yayoi culture (300 B.C.–A.D. 300), in which rice horticulture and bronze artifacts first appeared, with new cultural influences out of Korea and Siberia. One of the largest of the *kofun* burials is that of fifth-century Emperor Nintoku. His burial mound was 120 feet high and 1500 feet long.

The archeological and later historical documents of the early times describe the Kofun-period elites as horse-riding, armored, sword- and bow-wielding warriors who organized themselves into military clans. They quickly dominated the Yayoi cultures and laid the foundation of the latter-day rise of the samurai.

The *kofun* burials featured a small object called a *magatama* (curved jewel) which looks very much like a stylized bear claw. The sword, bronze mirror, and *magatama* make up the Three Imperial Treasures of modern Japan, the heart and soul of the Japanese people, and these three items are first found together during the time of the Kofun cultures.

It is interesting to note that during the same time the military elites of the Japanese Kofun period were forming the basis of the modern Japanese state, Clovis, war chief of the Salian Franks, was setting the stage for the rise of modern France through military successes in Europe. As the Kofun warriors rode into battle on their war horses, the Maya of Central America were building their great cities in the New World.

In 792, at the beginning of the Heian period, Prince Kammu instituted the "Stalwart Youth" system in which the young sons of high-ranking families were recruited as a permanent military corps to strengthen the ranks of the lower-level foot soldiers. The Stalwart Youth, like the elites of the Kofun period centuries before, were mounted, wore armor, and carried long swords and bows and arrows. Two years later, Kammu, after establishing Kyoto as his capital, built a special facility for martial arts training called the Butokuden or "Hall for the Training of the Virtues of the Warrior Way." Today there are such facilities in all major Japanese cities.

The gearing up of the proto-samurai class led to the final defeat of the aboriginal Japanese Ainu, who until that time had foiled the efforts of the Japanese ruling classes to remove them permanently from the main island of Honshu. The defeat of the Ainu proved the value of the warrior class and provided the basis of the title *shogun*, which means "Barbarian-defeating General."

The word *samurai* comes from a Japanese verb form meaning "to serve." Originally it meant a military retainer attached to a noble lord, or *daimyo*—very similar to the root of the English word *knight*. To be a samurai, one must serve, otherwise one is merely a *ronin*, or masterless warrior, a cloud drifting with no roots and no direction.

The samurai must be understood as much more than merely swords for hire although some of them, of course, were exactly that. I am speaking of the best of their type, the ideal to which modern *budoka* aspire. The samurai controlled the evolution of the infra-structure of the modern Japanese state. They designed and built roads, castles, gardens, bridges, dams, and harbors; enacted laws; maintained order at markets and on the highways; and patronized the great artists of their time. Many wrote poetry, painted, and sculpted.

Perhaps most important for the culture of modern Japan, the samurai evolved a code of behavior that became the model for much of contemporary Japan's concepts of etiquette, polite behavior, and manhood. The West experienced a similar pattern when the code of the European knights, chivalry (the code of horsemen), became the basis of modern Western male gentlemanly behavior. What made the samurai other than merely highly trained killers was the code of behavior that guided their lives—that, among others things, told them when it was proper to draw their weapons and when it was not.

In 1899 Japanese scholar and educator Nitobe Inazo was carrying out research in Europe when he was asked a very important question by his host, a Belgian judge. Nitobe recalls (Nitobe, 1979: Author's Preface):

>...our conversation turned during one of our rambles to the subject
>of religion. "Do you mean to say" asked the venerable professor,
>"that you have no religious instruction in your schools?" On my
>replying in the negative he suddenly halted in astonishment, and in

a voice which I shall not easily forget, he repeated "No religion! How do you impart moral education?" The question stunned me at the time. I could give no ready answer, for the moral precepts I learned in my childhood days, were not given in schools; and not until I began to analyze the different elements that formed my moral notions, did I find that it was bushido that breathed them into my nostrils.

Bushido has no Bible, no Koran, no singular "Holy Book of Bushido" to which all may turn for instruction. Rather, it is a code of behavior bequeathed to the members of the Japanese warrior class over many centuries through the example of seniors and teachers, constant exhortations to lead a brave, honorable, and moral life, and through poems, songs, and various works of art. Nitobe's reading of bushido is relatively modern. Earlier works like the *Hagakure* (Hidden in the Leaves), however, reflect the basic model of knightly behavior outlined by Nitobe as a code of internally consistent virtues.

The framework of bushido was firmly etched during the early education of the samurai youth, both male and female. The goal of education was to build stalwart character, and it was said to be built upon three principles: *chi* (wisdom), *jin* (benevolence), and *yu* (courage). Emphasis was placed on literacy, at least a nodding acquaintance with some of the Chinese (particularly Confucian) classics, and the ability to wield the writing brush with skill and spirit. Specific curricula included everything from literature, history, calligraphy, ethics, and military strategy and tactics to weapons practice, with a special focus on fencing, archery, spear fighting, horsemanship, and empty-handed self-defense. Various noble clans also had many secret techniques and curricula which they guarded for their own use and enrichment.

The sword, capable of cutting through gun barrels, was the ultimate weapon during its time, but it was much more than that. It was seen as a living thing, with a name, a personality, a particular history. It could be insulted, an act that would be taken as a personal insult by the samurai owning the weapon. Its spirit could be invoked for protection during sickness, childbirth, and times of grave danger. Its bright sheen, elegant shape, deadly potential, and beauty were seen as a model for samurai life. There was (and still is) an elaborate system of etiquette involved in handling swords, cleaning them, passing them from one person to another, and inspecting the blade of one belonging to someone else. The sword was a symbol of rank and prerogative. It was a work of art. It was a creation shared by the swordmaker and the gods. And yet it was rarely employed. In fact, the highest ideals of sword behavior were captured in such sayings as "The best won victory is that obtained without shedding blood" and "A sword in the scabbard is a jewel of great price."

One of the most objectionable aspects of bushido to the Westerner is the custom of *seppuku* (ritual disembowelment). Often erroneously called *harakiri* (literally, "belly cutting"), *seppuku* was a legal ceremonial institution for the samurai used particularly to protest breaches of honor. When one's honor was irretrievably destroyed, the samurai believed that the taking of one's own life was justified. Sometimes *seppuku* was preceded by *kataki uchi,* or revenge against a person or persons believed to be responsible for the lethal assault on one's honor. The very high value placed on honor was the typical background cause of the act of ritual suicide.

The samurai class included women, of course. They, like the males, were taught to be strong, stoic, honorable, and skillful with weapons. Their special weapon was the *kaiken* (long-bladed dagger). It was their sword, with which they were to defend their life and honor, exact revenge against attacks on their honor, and if it was necessary, commit *seppuku.* Samurai women also specialized, as previously noted, in the use of the Japanese halberd, the naginata.

Japanese history and legend present many examples of female samurai in action. For example, in the twelfth century, Tora Gozen of Oiso, a noted swordswoman, assisted the Soga clan in *kataki uchi.* During the same period, Miyagino and her sister Shinobu, brandishing war swords, fought a government official who had executed their father.

Tomoe Gozen was probably the most famous woman samurai in Japan's feudal history. In one battle she fought the war chief of the attacking force, Uchida Ieyoshi, and decapitated him, after which she killed several of his men. In another battle, after hours of fierce struggle, she was one of only seven warriors left standing. There is a stirring account of her defense of a bridge using her naginata against a hoard of attackers. Shizuka Gozen, mistress of the great general Minamoto Yoshitsune, often rode with her lover in battle. Hojo Masaki, wife of the first Minamoto shogun, rode with her husband many times, acting as one of his generals.

As to the values that were desired in the character of the samurai, Nitobe first mentions *rectitude*, the virtue of deciding on a course of action based on reason and then steadfastly following through with it. A Western folk hero, Davy Crockett, espoused a similar notion when he advised, "Make sure you are right, and then go right on ahead." The Japanese considered the label *gishi* (man of rectitude) as an indicator that the one so named was a master of learning and an artist of the highest caliber. It is obvious that one could not function as a warrior without this virtue; therefore, great pains were taken to instill it in the young.

However, what is the basis of a reasonable decision to act? What was the samurai supposed to be reasoning about? Nitobe states that the answer is *justice*. If the cause is unjust, then no act of the warrior is a virtue, according to bushido.

Valor is rectitude's twin, writes Nitobe. Valor is the courage to act when *right reason*, or *giri*, has concluded that an injustice has been committed. *Giri* also means duty on a grand scale; duty to one's parents, one's teachers, one's nation. Nitobe says, "...for what else is duty than what right reason demands and commands us to do."

The *spirit of daring* suggests that one is capable of performing well under stressful and dangerous conditions and, in fact, enjoying it. This alone, however, is not a virtue because if the daring act is committed for an unworthy cause, justice and right reason are not served; and if death occurs, all one has achieved is a "dog's death." The act of *courage* appears when one's daring act serves the cause of righteousness, of justice. Significantly enough, the key to a life of courage and one of the marks of a successful student of the martial ways is *endurance*. Survival for a warrior is necessary if they are to fulfill their function of service. The building of character does not demand quality at the outset so much as simple endurance, the ability to keep coming, for it is in that virtue that the others are built. It is noteworthy that the main basis for ranking in budo is seniority.

Nitobe notes (pp. 31-36) that according to Bushido, *benevolence, love, affection, sympathy,* and *nobility of feeling* were regarded as the highest attributes of the soul. The samurai were taught that a balance between rectitude and stern justice was essential to a balanced life. *Bushi no nasaki,* "the tenderness of the warrior," was a trait necessary to cultivate, according to bushido.

Gentle manners were taught to the warrior class. The warriors were encouraged to study music and poetry. In music they were urged to master the *biwa,* a lute-like instrument, as opposed to the more martial drums or trumpets.

Everyone of any education was a poet or a would-be poet. Not infrequently, a marching soldier might be seen to halt, take his writing utensils from his belt, and compose an ode. Such poems were often found after a battle in the helmets or armor of slain warriors.

It is said in Japan that budo begins and ends with *politeness.* But Bushido also added that politeness was not a virtue if it was motivated only by a fear of offending good taste. Nitobe writes (p. 37) that true politeness should be the outward manifestation of a sympathetic regard for the feelings of others. The stress on polite behavior was such that manners became an art form. Bowing, walking, sitting, standing, table manners, the serving of tea, and the shooting of an arrow all permitted the artistic expression of formal manners.

Bushido's concept of manners assumes that politeness has power. The school of etiquette of the Ogasawara clan taught that "the end of all etiquette is to so cultivate your mind that even when you are quietly seated, not the roughest ruffian can dare make onset on your person." Gracefulness represented economy of force. Fine manners indicated power in repose.

Nitobe states, however, (pp. 43-47), that politeness is a farce if it lacks *veracity,* or truthfulness. Lying was considered cowardly by the samurai. *Bushi no ichi gon,* the word of a samurai, was sufficient guarantee for the truthfulness of an assertion. The noble warrior's word carried such weight that promises were generally made and fulfilled without a written pledge, which would have been deemed quite beneath his dignity. It was not that lying was seen as a sin, but rather that it was considered a weakness and as such highly dishonorable.

Honor is a vivid consciousness of personal dignity and worth, says Nitobe (p. 50). It was centered in defense of the reputation of one's family, oneself, one's nation, and one's reputation. If honor was violated, the samurai would experience shame, a virtue which was regarded as one of the earliest indications of moral consciousness.

Honor was a dangerous virtue in that any infringement upon it required retribution; therefore, the samurai also insisted that *patience* and *forgiveness* must always be considered when matters of violated honor were being considered. They constantly repeated that overreaction to perceived infringements upon one's honor was dishonorable. A contemporary version of the correct way to consider attacks against honor is found in the story of a Western karatedoka traveling by bus with a karatedo master in Tokyo. As they were leaving the bus at their stop, a man impatient in quitting the bus pushed the karatedo master out of his way. The teacher did nothing, but the student was outraged that his master had been treated in such a fashion. "Aren't you going to do something?" he said to his teacher. The master replied, "Do you kick every dog that barks at you?"

Mencius, a Confucian scholar who had a tremendous impact on the evolution of budo, wrote, "Though you denude yourself and insult me, what is that to me? You cannot defile my soul with your outrage." One Japanese sage said, "When others speak all manner of evil things against you, return not evil for evil, but rather reflect that you were not more faithful in the discharge of your duties." Another writes, "To bear what you think you cannot bear is truly to bear." The samurai with hair-trigger emotions, ready to flash into martial reactions at any slight to his honor, was not seen as an admirable character in bushido; he was merely dangerous.

Loyalty was greatly respected in the code of the warriors, but the samurai were not expected to be loyal to a leader who asked them to violate the code of chivalrous honor. Nitobe continues (p. 56):

"Bushido did not require us to make our conscience the slave of any lord or king . . . . A man who sacrificed his own conscience to the capricious will or fancy of a sovereign was despised as a cringling."

It is clear that *self-control* is a paramount virtue in bushido. It was considered unmanly for a samurai to betray his emotions on his face. Notice that it was not unmanly to have emotions, just bad form to unintentionally reveal them to others. Self-control was important mainly as a method not to disrupt the harmony or peace of others by a display of personal emotion. "He shows no sign of joy or anger," Nitobe notes (p. 69), was an expression used in describing a person of admirable character.

An oft-repeated story tells of a starving samurai who comes upon some simple farmers eating their meager lunch by the side of the road. Knowing that the poor peasants would automatically feel the duty to give him their food, he quickly carved a toothpick from a twig and walked past them picking his teeth as if he had just eaten.

Nitobe's book, *Bushido*, was his attempt to interpret the code of the Japanese warrior for Westerners. But with "The Regulations of Imagawa Ryoshun" by General Imagawa Sadayo (1325–1420) and "The Wall Inscriptions" by General Nabeshima Naoshige (1538–1618), we can hear the voices of the samurai communicating with their own kind about proper budo behavior.

Imagawa Sadayo was a noted general and strategist, the military governor of Kyushu as well as an author of historical texts, travel diaries, and poetry. He composed his "Regulations" in 1412 at the request of his younger brother (Wilson, 1982:57-65).

The Regulations of Imagawa Ryoshun

Without knowledge of learning, one will ultimately have no military victories. Cormorant fishing and falconing are pleasures that uselessly destroy life. They are forbidden. It is forbidden to pass the death sentence on a man who has committed a minor crime without full investigation. It is forbidden to use favoritism and excuse a man who has committed a major crime. It is forbidden to bring about one's own excessive prosperity by means of exploiting the people and causing the destruction of shrines.

It is forbidden to tear down one's ancestors' family temples and pagodas, thereby embellishing one's own domicile. It is forbidden to forget the great debt of kindness one owes to his master and ancestors and thereby make light of the virtues of loyalty and filial piety. It is forbidden that one should, acting disrespective of the Way of Heaven, attach little importance to his duties to his master and be overly attentive to his own business. It is forbidden to be indiscriminate of one's retainers good or evil actions and to distribute unjust rewards and punishments. Be mindful of the fact that, as you know the works of your retainers, the master knows yours in the same way. It is forbidden to disrupt the relationships of other people and to make others' anguish your own pleasure. It is forbidden to put others' profit at a loss and, recklessly embracing one's own ambition, increase one's own power. It is forbidden to be disregardful of one's own financial status, and to live either too far above or below it. It is forbidden to have contempt for wise retainers and prefer flatterers, and to have one's actions be influenced by these considerations. One should not be envious of someone who has prospered by unjust deeds. Nor should he disdain someone who had fallen while adhering to the path of righteousness. It is forbidden to be given up to drinking and carousing and, in gambling and the like, to forget one's family duties. It is forbidden to be prideful of one's own cleverness. When a person comes to one's home, it is forbidden to feign illness and thus avoid meeting him. It is forbidden to enjoy one's own tranquility, and to retire a man without adding to him some stipend. It is forbidden to be excessive in one's own clothing and armor, while his retainers go about shabbily. It is forbidden to erect barriers within one's own domain and thus cause distress to travelers both coming and going. From the time one is young, he should associate with companions who are upright, and not even temporarily be taken in by friends of low character, for just as water will conform to the shape of the vessel that contains it, so will a man follow the good and evil of his companions.

If one would know the heart of the master, he should look to the companions whom the master loves. To prefer friends who are superior to him, and to avoid those who are his inferiors, is the wisdom of the good man. One must never depart from the Ways of both Warrior and Scholar.

As for the "Wall Inscriptions" of Nabeshima Naoshige, they are found in the third chapter of the famous samurai text, *Hagakure*, a guide written by Yamamoto Tsunetomo, a retainer of Lord Nabeshima's grandson Mitsushige (Wilson, 113-19).

Lord Nabeshima's Wall Inscriptions

Intelligence is the flower of discrimination. There are, however, many examples of the flower blooming but not bearing fruit. The arts are difficult to master by one's self. When one is unable to produce good judgement, he will for the most part do injury to himself. Encourage and listen well to the words of your subordinates. It is well known that gold lies hidden underground.

Faith is for the cleansing of one's mind, and should not be acted upon so as to disturb the minds of others. Prayer is the hedge that protects this flower. Coming up in the world should be done in the same way as ascending a stairway. Great events should be considered lightly. Do all things with patience. When affairs are carried out lackadaisically, seven out of ten will turn out badly. In a fight, one should be rough and reckless. Not so in everyday affairs.

No matter whether a person belongs to the upper or lower ranks, if he has not put his life on the line at least once he has cause for shame. Everyone should personally know exertion as it is known in the lower classes.

In the following, "The Last Statement of Torii Mototada" (Wilson, 120-24), a samurai who knows death is near as he observes his castle being surrounded by an overwhelming force of his enemy, writes to his son: "I will stand off the forces of the entire country here, and, without even one-hundredth of the men necessary to do so, will throw up a defense and die a resplendent death." His message is summarized in the last paragraph of his missive when the samurai father advises his son:

Be first of all prudent in your conduct and have correct manners, develop harmony between master and retainers, and have compassion on those beneath you. Be correct in the degree of rewards and punishments, and let there be no partiality in your degree of intimacy with your retainers. The foundation of man's duty as a man is in "truth." Beyond this, there is nothing to be said.

The samurai teachers left many pieces of advice concerning proper warrior conduct in terse inscriptions on hanging scrolls (*kakejiku*), ceramic pieces, screens, letters, and books, sometimes including quotations from Chinese sources. The following offer a sample (Wilson.):

> If a general who is to maintain the province does not have a special consciousness, his task will be a difficult one to attain. His attitude must not be the same as the ordinary man's. Firstly, he must be correct in manners and etiquette, must not let self-interest into government, and must take care of the common people.
> —Kuroda Nagamasa (1568–1623)

> There are no weak soldiers under a strong general.
> —from the *San Lueh*

> Avoid the enemy's strength, strike at his weakness.
> —From Sun Tzu's *Art of War*

> High living is like drinking poisoned sake: it is unthinkable.
> —from the *Tso Ch'uan*

> One should attend to his warriors as he would to his own thirst.
> —in the *Chun Ch'uan*

> One should not turn his back on reproof. In the words of the ancients, "Good medicine is bitter to the mouth, but has effect on the disease."
> —Takeda Nobushige (1525–61)

> The arts of peace and the arts of war are like the two wheels of a cart which, lacking one, will have difficulty in standing.
> —Kuroda Nagamasa (1568–1623)

> What is called the Way of the Warrior is not a matter of extolling the martial arts above all things and becoming a scaremonger.
> —Kuroda Nagamasa (1568–1623)

Also, the various martial arts traditions (*ryu*) bequeathed to their adherents their own words of wisdom. The following, "Songs of the Way of the Spear" of the Hozoin school, which date to about 1600, and the verses of the Saburi School, which date to the same period, are examples (Leggett, 1978:165-67).

Songs of the Way of the Spear
By what I did yesterday, I win today
This is the virtue of practice.
Remember the old saying,
The plan for a day is a cock's crow,
The plan for a life is something serious.
In the knightly arts, first see that you yourself are right,
And after that think of defeating an opponent.
The unskilled man does not know his own faults.
And yet dreams vainly of defeating another.
The Way is first of all about one's own defects;
After that, you can defeat others.
Without knowing the stains and faults in one's own self,
How empty to dream of victory over others!
In the knightly arts, if a man's will is right
There is no doubt of his ultimate victory.
Don't think to win just by force;
There is hard in the soft, soft in the hard.
"Softness is just weakness," some say;
But know there is a difference between softness and weakness.
When making an attack, do not be careless;
There is a waiting in action, an action in waiting.
In all the turns of the combat, never must one get controlled by
 the enemy. That is what is always to be remembered.
In a contest, you must be aware of the distance and the timing;
But do not lose sight of the awareness which is beyond them.
When you penetrate deep to the simple awareness,
You will experience the state of being and non-being.
It is like a stream, which when flowing is pure;
If it stands still, it becomes putrid.

*Against a strong opponent, though you lose still you get
  something out of it;*
Do not think always in one straight line.
In a contest, first control your own mind;
Only after that think about technique.
If you have control of your mind, be careful not to lose it;
Hold the mind firm, and then make the thrust.
The hands waiting, the feet active without flagging;
Let the heart be that of a waterbird swimming.
When the short body and the long spear are a unity,
The enemy finds no opening to strike.

Verses of the Saburi School
There is no village where the moon does not shine,
But it is clear in the hearts of men of poetry.
*Though one thinks, "I have thrown away the world, my body is
  naught,"*
Still when the snow falls, the night is cold.
*The samurai who is gentle in his benevolence and in his duty and
  in his bravery,*
He is not burnt up in fire nor drowned in water.
Though a man is well-equipped and strong and great,
If he does not know the Way of the knight, he is as a stick or stone.
The beach pine has no voice;
When the wind blows, it sings.
*The water does not think of giving it lodging Nor the moon of
  lodging there.*
How clear the reflection!
The heart which can hear the frost forming on a cold night,
When confronted with an enemy, will snatch the victory.

You may wonder why I have spent so much time with ancient texts
about warrior behavior when the theme of this book deals with contemporary martial arts practice in Japan. It is because the code of the
warrior, for many centuries, has answered all the questions that have
arisen out of the context of warrior training. Behave in terms of
bushido at all times, and you will never be wrong in a traditional

Japanese martial arts school. You may at times appear old-fashioned to young Japanese students, but you are already a *gaijin* (foreigner) and therefore already interestingly peculiar. What is important is that your budo teachers will understand your behavior and appreciate it. And even more important is that living the code of the warrior with full consciousness will make you a better person, and therefore a better citizen, capable of serving the cause of peace and harmony in your family and community.

The Japanese code of the warrior evolved through time, adapting to changing economic and political conditions while maintaining the internal balances that made the noble warrior recognizable through the centuries. Since that is the case, you should not see the code of the warrior as being written in stone and adopt it blindly, but rather adapt it to the reality you find yourself in with one guiding question: how can my behavior at this point in time promote peace?

Some of the codes expressed by certain ancient samurai leaders have little in them that one should find attractive as a model for behavior. For example, Kato Kiyomasa (1562–1611), whose ferocity in battle led the Koreans to call him the "Devil General," promulgated the following ideas about the proper behavior of samurai under his authority (Wilson, 130-32):

> A samurai who practices dancing—which is outside of the martial arts—should be ordered to commit seppuku. A person who loves beautification where it is unnecessary is fit for punishment. Reading Chinese poetry, linked verse, and waka is forbidden. One will surely become womanized if he gives his heart knowledge of such elegant, delicate refinements. If there is anyone who finds these conditions difficult to fulfill, he should be dismissed, an investigation should be quickly carried out, it should be signed and sealed that he was unable to mature in the Way of manhood, and he should be driven out.

And always remember that bushido, read in terms of nationalistic pride, blind loyalty to leaders and country, and military expansionism was a contributing factor leading to Japan's disastrous defeat in World War II. All codes can be manipulated, and all codes can manipulate. Be careful. Keep your eyes open and think about what you are prepared to accept as a code of reasonable behavior. Find what is good and useful and leave the rest.

Like soldiers everywhere, the samurai did not spend most of their time fighting but rather serving the ends of peace in their territories which, of course, was the best situation for the lords who hired them: men who made a living off local commerce, trade, farming, and taxes. Warfare meant that the lord was losing money. Peace meant that he was amassing it. If you were a member of the landed gentry, what would you reward your retainers for doing: making war or making peace?

All of the ideal behaviors described here are to be considered as rules of thumb. The most important rule is to act harmoniously with the group of which you are a member. Teachers, even those of the same style, have different attitudes about what constitutes correct behavior. When in doubt, study the behavior of the most senior students in the dojo.

Dojo: The Place of the Way

Japanese martial-arts practice facilities, known as dojo (literally, "place of the way"), come in all shapes and sizes. The primal base of the term suggests a place where meditation is practiced, a place of honor and strength, a castle of sorts. Again, the name the Japanese give to such a place is important in understanding what your teachers expect you to be intent on practicing. In fact, it is always insightful to delve into the meanings implied by the terms the Japanese budoka use to describe the inner and outer aspects of their practice. You will be training in a dojo, not a gym, not a weight room, not an exercise facility. You will be training in a place, no matter how humble the physical appearance, which you are supposed to honor and respect, and in which you are to practice the refinement of your body, spirit, and behavior.

Japanese martial arts dojo are so varied in their approaches to teaching, in their reaction to the presence of foreigners, and in the precise nature of expected junior-senior, teacher-student relationships that simply having studied the same style in the West may not have prepared you for what you will face in Japan.

Unless you are already locked in to practice at your style's *hombu* through letters of introduction or prearranged living quarters, you will need to visit potential dojo first to ensure that the nature of what is happening fits your level of acceptability. Even if you have signed on at one dojo you really should take the opportunity of your time in Japan to visit, observe, and perhaps even practice, with other budoka. As Japan's greatest swordsman, Miyamoto Musashi, often said, "Study all arts."

When visiting a new dojo, dress well. I usually wore a suit and tie to observe at a dojo. The gesture was appreciated but very outdated. It might be better to say "Dress as if you are going for a job interview." In a sense, you are. I also paid attention to maintaining a quiet and dignified demeanor throughout the practice. Although you may not be aware of it, you are being observed. An old samurai adage states, "Behave as if even the walls have eyes." If you really want to make a good impression, don't lean against the back of your chair as you observe, don't cross your legs, don't fidget and look about, and don't laugh and talk with those sitting near you.

After class I approached the senior student, usually identified by the place he or she takes when the students are seated facing the sensei. This very important person sits to the right of all other students. I would always express my gratitude for being allowed to observe and compliment the style and the quality of the students. Usually an introduction to the sensei would follow, and if I had passed the first test—sitting quietly and acting politely—I would be invited to practice with the group. This invitation will be light and friendly in nature and will not require a potentially life-changing decision to be made on the spot.

How do you know if you should accept the invitation? How do you decide if the dojo is the one for you? There are four questions you should ask yourself. First, do you trust the style? Does it look sound in terms of fundamentals? Do you believe it could be practically applied? Does it make you feel excited and happy to watch it? Does it touch your artistic sense? I've noticed that when you hit the right art, you will have a vague feeling of familiarity. You will feel as if a homecoming is at hand.

Second, do you trust the teacher? Does the teacher inspire your confidence and respect? Do you like the manner in which the lessons are conveyed? Are they clear in their presentation? Do they treat their students with respect? Are they in control of the class? Do they express a calm sense of competence?

Third, do you trust the students? After all, you will mainly be physically involved with your fellow students if you join the dojo. Do they show respect and care while training together? Do they respect their teacher? The dojo? Does their relative skill reflect well on their teacher? Are they knowledgeable about dojo etiquette? How do the senior students relate to the juniors?

Fourth, what do you feel about what you have seen? The preceding basics of observation of the style, the teacher, and students should elicit an overall feeling of either acceptance or rejection. You must learn to trust your gut feelings. Usually, when you line up your various experiences for evaluation, one will clearly stand out from the others and it may be for no apparent reason. It is a lot safer to go this way than to join a dojo because it looks good but somehow doesn't "feel right."

If you go to both visit and practice at a dojo you are interested in joining, there are a few rules that are important to keep in mind. Regardless of your rank, wear a white belt and sit in the junior-most position among the dojo students. Even if you are asked to take a more senior position, when placed next to dojo students of your rank, sit slightly back instead of even with the senior students of the dojo. These acts are statements of humility, a highly prized budo value, and they also indicate that you have both a fairly refined notion of dojo etiquette as well as self-effacing humility.

It is also customary to pay a "mat fee" if you are visiting a dojo and also practicing. The price is symbolic of your awareness of debt repayment and should probably range from about three to five dollars. Often, even if you offer to pay a mat fee, the dojo manager will refuse to accept it. Don't fail, however, to make the offer. Not to do so is mildly insulting and indicates your lack of knowledge of budo behavior.

Some of the dojo where I either observed martial arts training or practiced myself were no more than rooms over small businesses. Sometimes businesses will allow *budoka* to use their space in the evenings when most martial arts training takes place. Some businesses, in fact, have dojo facilities built in for the use of their employees and their families. Dojo can also be located in college or university gymnasiums. Regardless, when you practice budo correctly, wherever you are is to be treated as a dojo. It may be a space in a local park. It may be in a garage. It may be the beach. It may be your teacher's garden or even rooms in his or her home.

One dojo in which I practiced was located on the grounds of a large Shinto temple (Gokoku Jinja) and another in a budokan ("place of practice of the warrior ways") that was adjacent to a three-acre Zen garden in Ohori Koen, a local park. As I came to appreciate the cultural context in which budo training took place, as well as the meditative and spiritual aspects of the training, I found deep pleasure in approaching and leaving the budokan through the precincts of the temple or by way of the paths and bridges of the Zen garden. The stillness, order, and beauty of such places provided for me a perfect beginning and ending to budo practice.

Budokan are found in almost all major cities and for the visiting martial arts student they are a mecca. The one in which I trained is a facility the size of a professional basketball arena. In the training area hardwood floors covered about three-fourths of the space with mats covering the rest. The building included offices and meeting rooms, changing rooms, lockers, toilets, showers, etc. On the grounds of the Fukuoka Budokan, one could find sumo practice rings as well as a beautiful kyudo shooting range.

I practiced Muso-ryu jodo and kyudo at the Fukuoka Budokan. Jodo classes met three times a week. At one end of the large wooden floor area a kendo class of over forty young men and women practiced while at the other end a large judo group held down one corner of the floor as an *aiki jujutsu* group worked in the other. Sometimes the middle area, where the *jodoka* worked, was shared with a Shorinji Kempo club. I remember the first time I walked onto the jodo practice area because of the strange texture beneath my feet. The floor, which looked like a typical wooden basketball surface, was covered in round dents as if someone had gone over just about every square inch with a ballpeen hammer, leaving thousands of uniform round impressions.

106

I remember thinking at that moment about the zeal with which my high school basketball coach protected the surface of his floor. "Jones! No street shoes on the gym floor!" This, I thought as I touched the dimpled floor, would have killed him.

The cause of the deformed surface area became clear about twenty minutes into class. Muso-ryu jodo practices an overhead strike with the short staff which is supposed to hit the ground, slide forward, and then come up in a scooping motion. We were literally practicing on a surface created by countless thousands of such strikes. Although I never could remove the shocked look of my old basketball coach from my mind every time I looked at that floor, I came in time to feel a kind of connection with the past jodo players who had struck hard enough with their oak staves to drive deep dents into a hardwood athletic floor.

The sounds of the martial arts have deeply interested me since a Japanese teacher once talked to me about *ashi-mimi* (literally: "foot-ear"). He noted that listening to the footsteps of attackers coming from behind you, for example, had to be practiced and used to time your defense. He observed that warriors listened to birds, crickets, frogs, the wind, and the depth of echo in a darkened room as part of the techniques that could save their lives.

One of the most novel sounds I heard at the budokan came my second day of jodo practice. As I was dressing, I heard a series of three sounds coming from the far end of the floor. It sounded like a *kiai*, followed by the thud of a foot or fist striking padding, which in turn was followed by a peculiar "pock" sound. I tried to picture the source of the sounds but had no success. I turned to find the Shorinji Kempo students sparring, dressed in a strange set of protective gear. The upper body was covered by what looked like a large baseball catcher's chest protector, while the head was protected by a plastic bubble-like mask. The students were practicing a combination in which a strike with *kiai* to the solar plexus was followed rapidly by a strike to the face. Hence, shout-thud-and-pock as the plastic bubble clicked back into shape after being hit.

For Westerners, one of the interesting aspects of the many styles practicing on the same large floor was that dressing and undressing for practice took place in the same room where the various arts were being practiced. You could go to a private room to change if you wished, but most of the Japanese practitioners changed on the floor along the edges of the practice area. You had to be very subtle in taking your street clothes off and putting your practice uniform on with the utmost modesty in a mixed group. It took as much concentration on my part to change clothes correctly and with decorum as it took to learn to wield a short staff with some small degree of correctness. Pay attention to local behavior. I also saw dojo were no one dressed on the dojo floor. Sometimes it had to do with available facilities.

The dojo may also be located in ancient buildings as was the central Muso-ryu Jodojo in Fukuoka. Many of them are beautifully landscaped and gardened. Obviously good physical training ultimately rests on one's ability to become immune to surroundings and mental and physical distractions, but there is a lot more to budo practice than the moments in which one is sweating and breathing hard. The antiquity and beauty of some dojo are inspiring. These are the kinds of things you will remember after your time in Japan is over and you have returned home. In your practice facilities in your home town you can sweat just as much as you can in Japan, but the environment is not the same. Try to understand your training in terms of the entire context of your existence while in Japan. There is much, much more to budo than what can be experienced with the physical body.

There are a number of types of dojo in Japan. Since I was working for the Japanese Ministry of Education while in Japan, I spent a lot of time on college and university campuses. The sound of *kiai* always accompanied the late afternoon shadows as the various budo clubs went through their after-school workouts. I could hear the thunk of arrows being shot by the Kyudo club or the clash of *shinai* on armor as the kendo club practiced for their next meet. The shouted cadence of the karatedo instructors and the synchronized *kiai* of the karatedo clubs mixed with the sound of bodies crashing to the mat in the judo and aikido club facilities. Even the nearby high school baseball team sent *kiai* into the air, encouraging each other as they ran wind sprints and practiced hitting and fielding. Where I lived, the karatedo and kyudo groups worked outside in good weather, while the judo, aikido and kendo clubs usually practiced in the gymnasiums on the campus.

A typical pattern for the university clubs seemed to be that a senior instructor would work with students or observe maybe once or twice a week, performing similar duties at other campuses, while most of the daily practice was led by senior students.

The college and university clubs are notorious for the rigor of their practices. I observed several college aikido clubs which practiced their characteristic rolls and break falls, not on mats, but on the wooden floor of the gymnasium. The excesses one occasionally heard about—beatings administered by senior students to junior students being a typical example—generally occurred, when they happened at all, in the college and university clubs, and some universities had worse reputations than others. I mention this in my role as a guide but I want to immediately emphasize that such occurrences were rare, although anyone who has spent any time at all practicing in Japan will sooner or later hear about it. It seemed to me to have the same general tone as when from time to time American news media report on an attack by members of a high school or college football team on someone they deem unworthy for whatever reason. It is disgusting and cowardly behavior and thankfully rare.

The budokan provide an excellent opportunity for foreign students to begin practice of various martial arts and to observe many others in their workouts. The instructors, in my experience, were some of the best in the area. The pride and honor of the city in which a particular budokan existed and the fact that the various arts were on public view led to only the best teachers taking part. Also, once a foreign student became known by attendance at budokan classes he or she was usually invited to practice at the particular style's central dojo located in the same town or someplace nearby.

There was one type of dojo I learned very quickly to avoid because I was not interested in having to protect myself against my dojo mates. If you visit a dojo where all of the students are young Japanese men with closely cropped hair and show the physical signs of being extremely well-conditioned and muscular, you might want to hesitate before walking onto the mat. As in the West, where one can find martial arts schools that specialize in full-contact fighting, as well as some version of "Karate for Christ," or claim to teach you "street" techniques, so too in Japan you will find a complex variety of clubs. Some are extremely right-wing and anti-Western. Again, this situation is rare, but it does exist. Some Westerners may find such a club intriguing and challenging in the extreme. I guess it depends how fond you are of your bones and teeth.

My favorite dojo were the ones comprised of males and females, old and young, beginners and advanced students. I was drawn to such places because my personal budo feeling had developed over a quarter-century of practice to draw me toward a feeling of family and personal warmth, civility and community. I felt that I ultimately learned more if I practiced with a senior student one moment, a youngster the next, and an elderly person the next. There comes a time in your training in which a feeling of something like love substitutes for the desire to use your classmates as punching bags. One of my teachers once told me that budo can satisfy all cravings and suggested that such power was one of its greatest dangers. In budo, you will get what you are looking for.

Sometimes you find dojo established near American military bases which serve Western service personnel who have a short hitch in a Japanese duty station. This is often the testing ground for a Japanese advanced senior student to serve as teacher. If you can learn to have the patience and physical and interpersonal skills to teach budo to a bunch of bored American sailors, you should probably be promoted another grade or two.

There are also dojo which, though not located near a military base, feature a Japanese teacher and a class made up of Westerners only. I know that it is difficult for some Westerners to enter another culture and immediately jump into its activities. Some people need a halfway house, a staging ground. Such dojo may give you the confidence you need to seek entry into a more traditional dojo. But also remember that the best dojo in the world is always the one composed of people you like and respect; the dojo's location and race of the teachers and students are of little importance in the long run.

Usually the best situation is to find a *hombu* (home dojo; headquarters) of a particular style. Usually at such places you will find the very best instructors and facilities, as well as classes designed specifically for foreigners of all flavors. Big central dojo almost always have children's classes, and sometimes special classes for dancers, actors, gymnasts, police officers, or people with particular physical disabilities.

The dojo is, among many other things, a battlefield on which you confront your worst enemy, the person who has caused you the most pain and difficulty in your life, the person you see in the mirror every morning when you awake. Be aware that your chief enemy will not fight fair. He or she brings a host of support troops that one of my old teachers called "hungry ghosts." These spirits live in your head and they will do their best to drive you from the battlefield. They may begin their attack even before you have taken the field. They might attempt to weaken your fighting spirit before the engagement. They say things like "Maybe you should reconsider this crazy notion of practicing traditional martial arts while in Japan. Maybe you should spend your time visiting temples, gardens, shrines and museums," or "You don't know the Japanese language so you won't really know what's going on," or "You're just going to make a fool of yourself. The Japanese have martial arts in their blood. You'll look like an idiot. They will kill you."

Even if you penetrate the outer perimeters of the hungry ghosts and breech the invisible walls to make it through a workout in the dojo, the hungry ghosts will come again. They'll whisper, "You're really awkward and clumsy at this," and "Your body hurts, your muscles are sore. What a stupid waste of time when you could be taking this once-in-a-lifetime opportunity in Japan to do some relaxing, enjoyable, and educational sightseeing." These are some of the strategies of your real enemy. In Asian martial culture there are dozens of versions of the saying, "To control one hundred men is hard. To control the self is harder still."

It is one of the ironies of the Way of the Warrior that the more difficulties you have to overcome—the haranguing of the hungry ghosts, the weakness of the body, the lack of natural athletic ability and inclination to fight—the luckier you are. All victories are judged relative to the quality of the opponent. All martial arts teachers have experienced the natural athlete who enters a dojo, displays beautiful physical technique in a short time, and then gradually fades away—

while the awkward, untalented student who tries and tries and refuses to give up attains honor. Remember that ranking in traditional budo is by seniority and not necessarily by skill alone. The poor physical student who has struggled in the great battle for years is worth more than the student who can physically perform the outer elements of his or her chosen art in a matter of a few months. All you have to do is survive over time to achieve honor and rank in traditional martial arts. My karatedo sensei commented on this by saying, "The father loves the ugly son best."

Another teacher explained the nature of practice and ranking in budo by likening it to a general reviewing his troops after a battle. The custom, even with modern heads of state, is to walk slowly before the troops and look at their faces. As battle follows battle, the general will recognize certain warriors whose faces appear before him time after time, battle after battle. Are they necessarily the very best of his warriors? No. Nor are they the very worst. Martial arts tends to select for tenacity. To succeed in the traditional dojo at those things which really matter is the simplest thing, and the hardest thing: *keep coming!* That's the only real secret, whether you practice martial arts in Japan or at home.

The dojo has a traditional spatial/symbolic structure. Areas of the dojo have specific meaning and usage. There are areas you should occupy and areas you should not occupy. There are ways of entering a traditional dojo and prescribed ways of leaving. None of this is truly a matter of life and death, by the way, but attention to the details of where you are at any particular moment is both a real necessity for a warrior who plans on living past the next several seconds as well as a means of quieting the debilitating babbling of the hungry ghosts. Notice that the ghosts are never where you really are. They are always trying to put your mind in everyplace *but* the present. That should give you hope in understanding how to defeat them. Also, always remember that the lessons of the dojo battlefield are abstract lessons that are meant to be expressed in your day-to-day life outside the precincts of the dojo. Don't mistake the finger pointing to the moon for the moon itself.

The spatial and directional symbols of the dojo are ancient, and are found in many cultures. Conceive of the four sides of the dojo practice area as a compass. As with a compass, the orienting direction is north. The north side of the dojo is called the "upper seat," or *kamiza*, It is the central focus of the dojo, reserved for instructors and honored guests.

The upper seat will often feature a slightly raised dais upon which may sit a flower arrangement or a *bonsai* tree or sword or drum, and behind which hangs a scroll (*kakejiku*) or a picture of the founder of the martial art practiced at the dojo. Sometimes, a Japanese flag may be hung in the area of the upper seat, and sometimes a rendering of the emblems of the art. There are many variations on how the upper seat is decorated. Sometimes all that is found on the north is a small conventional Shinto shrine, generally set high up on the north wall. This was the case, for example, at the *aikidojo* where I practiced in Fukuoka.

The symbolic role of the north as the place where the highest-ranking practitioner sits has, as noted earlier, many cross-cultural echoes. In China, t'ai chi ch'uan was sometimes called "Pole Star Boxing" (referring to the North Star), and the practitioners faced the north as they began the practice of their forms. North is widely seen as the source of danger or evil. The Pole Star Boxer faced north as a symbol of protection to those around him. Among the American Indians, the Kiowa Apache warriors stand in the north during their ritual dances as a symbol that they protect the south (women and children) from danger. In traditional Navaho culture, as in Japan, north was the direction of death. Deceased individuals, for example, were removed from the hogan, the traditional Navaho house, through the north wall.

The "lower seat," or *shimoza*, is located to the south. This is where the students sit. It is a location of youth, growth, hope, the future. It is sometimes said, "There is no teaching from the south." This saying has many meanings, but its basic sense is that students should not speak to each other or instruct each other during practice.

The "upper side" (*joseki*) is located to the east. This is where visitors sit. The space is also where the instructor sits if the *kamiza* is occupied by an honored guest. If the dojo is crowded, senior-ranking students will sit along the upper side; and during dojo testing, the examiners and those being tested typically will sit in a east-west alignment.

The upper side—east, the direction of the rising sun—is also associated with enlightenment. Some practitioners will, after students and teacher exchange bows at the beginning and ending of class, turn toward the east and bow in an act that symbolizes honoring *satori*, or enlightenment, the goal of many martial arts. Again, among the American Indians I have worked with, the east is the direction of wisdom and strength and is often the origin point of war gods, who are generally depicted as bright and shining young men.

The west is the "lower side" (*shimoseki*). It is a null space and is anciently symbolized as a place of night and darkness. In many cultures the direction the dead take to the afterlife is westward. The references are related to the poetic image of the setting sun as prelude to night.

The relationship of *kamiza* (north) and *shimoza* (south) will always pertain, whereas the function of the other directions may depend on the nature of the dojo structure. In one dojo at which I practiced, visitors sat not in the *joseki* but behind the students because that was the only possible place to sit in the small building. Likewise the compass directions are symbolic and the actual placement of the *kamiza*, the key to orienting everything else in the dojo, may simply be where it is most convenient given the space being occupied by the dojo practice area or mat.

A key relationship in all Japanese dojo is that between senior students (*sempai*) and junior students (*kohai*). The tenor of that relationship varies widely and its implications for you, an automatic *kohai*, or junior student, is primary. This is one of the things you should watch for when visiting the dojo of a style you might like to join. Senior students will naturally vary in terms of how they interpret their role.

In some cases I saw seniors mentoring juniors with friendliness and good humor. The seniors were clearly in charge and advanced and they used this advantage to train their charges with the decorum befitting a dojo. On the other hand, I saw dojo in which the seniors seemed more like bullies than mentors. I witnessed this only in various college and university clubs. but I was told that it existed elsewhere in other types of dojo.

I remember watching a college aikido class and being horrified at the way the juniors were treated. In most aikido classes the sensei will demonstrate a technique, perhaps offer some slight commentary, and then indicate that the students should select a partner and practice. Usually, one works with as many members of the class as is possible or practical. This is both polite and also good practice philosophy. However, in this dojo, after the sensei clapped his hands indicating that practice should begin, the juniors remained seated while the seniors, in order of seniority, selected their junior partners with a negligible wave of the hand and grunt. The junior was then thrown repeatedly and not given an opportunity to practice the throw on his senior partner. Further, at the end of class, the juniors remained seated while the seniors changed to street clothes. The last thing I saw before I walked out was the seniors throwing their sweat soaked *dogi* into the face of the formally seated juniors with the message: "Wash this and bring it back to me next time." I never went back, nor did I care to meet the sensei. That dojo was not teaching what I would wish to learn. Their physical technique was excellent. The spirit of the dojo, however, was full of violence, ego, and fear. It was a dark place. This dojo was not typical of aikido instruction by any means, but I mention it because it illustrates that it is imperative that you watch a class carefully and thoughtfully before you commit your mind and body to the dojo sensei and seniors.

The "spirit" of a dojo is directly related to the concept of training held by the sensei in charge. Ueshiba Morihei, founder of aikido, often commented that the attitude of the *aikidojo* should be joyous. He did not mean "not serious," and some of his dojo were called "Hell dojo." You will find that when you have arrived at the art that is right for you, however, that you will experience radiance and joy as a direct result of intense practice. Other budo teachers may see the dojo as a more grim situation than that envisioned by Master Ueshiba. Fredrick J. Lovret, a rightly well-respected Budoka, when discussing the differences between a "martial arts school" and a dojo, writes (Lovret, 1987:14-15):

"A school teaches techniques, as does a dojo. However, in a dojo, techniques are viewed as only a means to an end. The techniques must be mastered, but that is only the beginning, not the end, of study. The goal of a school is to teach a person new things; the goal of a dojo is to transform the person into something new. A school teaches how to kill; a dojo teaches how to die."

The key to the spirit of a dojo is always the sensei. This term is often erroneously used in the West to indicate a spiritual teacher, and students will sometimes inadvertently bow their heads and speak in hushed tones when they mention that sensei said this, or sensei did that. However, in Japan, you refer to the local pharmacist at the drugstore as "sensei." Your tennis coach is "sensei." When I was teaching in Japanese universities I was addressed as "Jones Sensei" by my students. The sensei is most important, but the sensei does not claim to be a saint or require that his students follow his way of life. You are not trying to become the sensei; you are trying to become *you.*

Yet it is definitely the case that the term for a teacher in Japan carries more weight than it does in the West. An old Chinese proverb states: "Thank the gods for giving you life, thank your parents for rearing you, and thank your teachers for everything else." The budo sensei is in charge at all times. Students never debate with a sensei. If the sensei holds up three fingers and says, "I am holding up two fingers," the proper response is "Yes, sensei!" The attitude of *nyunanshin* is required. Lovret (p. 15) writes:

"This means having a flexible spirit and being capable of being molded by the dojo. Becoming a *deshi* (inner student; disciple) requires that a person surrender his ego to the headmaster, the sensei. In effect, he says, 'Here I am. Do with me what you will.'"

The sensei might be seen as an object of meditation. His or her ego should not be at issue. He or she should be empty of such encumbrances. The sensei represents order and peace as well as the vagaries of everyday life. The sensei might be seen as "everyday life" incarnate, and your behavior while in the sensei's presence on the floor of the dojo reflects your sophistication in dealing abstractly with the highs and lows of living. Everyday life is the real target of your practice. You are not so much training to achieve an acceptable high-level roundhouse kick as you are training to acquire virtues that you may take into everyday life, virtues derived from the solid effort required to develop a passable roundhouse kick. Remember that you are to practice a "way," not a goal. Perhaps one could say that the way is the goal, which means that once you *truly* begin, you have already arrived. A Catholic saint named Catherine once said, "All the way to heaven is heaven." As one of my karatedo teachers once said, "Real karatedo is practiced in the world, not in the dojo."

I first recognized the "way" aspect of martial arts training when I had been in aikido for a few years. A hypnotist moved into the store next to our dojo. He specialized in helping musicians or typists, for example, accelerate their learning by hypnotizing them while they practiced. The music student, for example, would practice five minutes under hypnosis after which the hypnotist would offer the suggestion that he or she had, in fact, been practicing for over an hour. He had the data to support his contention that the skill level of the student rose significantly.

One evening he dropped by the *aikidojo* after his office closed and watched us practicing forward rolls, one of the more difficult aspects of aikido training for the beginner. After watching us for a while, he offered that he could hypnotize us while we practiced our rolls and break-falls, suggest to us that we had been practicing for an hour, and thereby accelerate our skill in falling. We were all interested, but on the way home that night it dawned on me that I wasn't so much interested in learning good falling and tumbling techniques as I was in the painful process of achieving that end. I found that I was interested in the "way" much more than the goal.

The martial arts of Japan might be seen in a very instructive way as abstract arts. It is their inner form and essence that is sought, not the outer glitz and showroom dress. The sensei may thunder and rage one day and play with you like an old grandfather the next. It is not real. No one on the street is going to be wearing a *dogi* or *hakama*, or attacking you with archaic weapons. The sensei invites you into an abstraction based around an historical reality called "the way of the warrior."

In that the sensei is "life," the student can never achieve a position in any way superior to the sensei. In gift-giving to the sensei, a very natural expression of the feeling of the student, one must be careful not to "burden" the sensei with a gift that he or she may not be able to repay either outright or in the role as sensei. I received a valuable lesson one time when I unknowingly gave my sensei a gift that was too much. He took the present, examined it with appreciation, and then handed it back to me saying, "I accept the spirit of your gift."

Remember that dojo are not created with a cookie cutter. They each reflect that nature of the art, and the teacher, students, and community in which they are found. Some dojo's "joyous" practice may be lightweight in the extreme, while some dojo feel like a school for demented thugs. These dojo philosophies will naturally determine the intensity and nature of training in that particular dojo.

Where does hard traditional training cross the line into sadism? This is a personal call. The line is fuzzy. When I was practicing Zen at Shofukuji in Fukuoka, the Zen sitting period included the experience of having a senior monk patrol the rows of sitting meditators with a *kyosaku* (a sword-length dowel shaved thin at one end and split) with which he would strike meditators who looked to him as if they needed it. Perhaps they were looking sleepy or maybe they were showing signs of tension in their shoulders and upper back.

This striking was ritualized and therefore predictable. The head monk would stop before a sitter, bow deeply, and strike the sitter three times on one side of the upper back and shoulder area and three times on the other, after which both sitter and striker would bow deeply to each other. This behavior is standard in most Zen temples and points, as strange as it may seem to Westerners, not to violence but to compassion. It is the coach's slap on the back as he fires up a player before sending him into the game. It is a wake-up call. It is a stimulating shock to nerve plexus which must be relaxed and functioning for efficient *zazen* (sitting meditation). It is also much more.

Sometimes a study of the cultural context of Zen training in Japan, for example, will enable one to judge if the training technique is acceptable and appropriate by Japanese standards. This will then allow the neophyte to choose whether he or she really wants to experience the sometimes harsh edges of training, even if it is traditionally acceptable. It is quite common for Westerners desirous of sampling Zen training to seek assurance that they won't be hit. What is a minor aspect of Zen training to the Japanese becomes a major focus for Westerners.

However, some martial arts styles really do want you to punch a tree until your knuckles are callused and hardened. Some teachers will assume that you will consider it an honor if they blacken your eye or choke you into unconsciousness. Some schools will suggest that you accept broken bones as a requisite of sincere practice. And some Westerners accept those conditions entirely. However, most do not, and I would hazard the guess that most Japanese do not either.

In a good dojo will your teachers ever yell at you, push you, cause you physical and psychological discomfort? The answer is yes, if you are lucky and try very hard. Also, remember that you have selected to train in martial arts, not flower arranging or the tea ceremony. It is also true that some martial arts, such as judo, kendo, aikido, and karatedo, lend themselves to potential harsh physical encounters with teachers or seniors, while others, such as iaido, jodo, and kyudo, provide much less potential for possible negative physical encounters.

The best gauge of what is acceptable behavior is found in a combination of educating yourself about the training methods of the art you wish to practice (remembering that the bottom line is the training of warriors), and your personal feelings about how much is too much for you. Whenever you feel the line has been crossed, I suggest you bow and walk away. There is no honor, for example, in allowing yourself to be brutalized by a teacher or senior student who may just happen to be a racist with a very bad attitude about foreigners. At the same time, be very careful that you do not massage feelings of indignation to excuse yourself from the challenge of martial arts training. As with almost all of the more subtle aspects of budo training, the answers are within you. Your job is to strive to perceive these inner truths with clarity. The bottom line is discovering your true self, not creating yet another false self.

When in the dojo, communicate with the eyes, subtle head shifts, and body movements rather than with what would be seen as too much verbal communication. Likewise, learn as quickly as possible to understand communications that may come to you in a slight raise of the shoulder or widening of the eyes. Controlling facial expression is very important. The samurai often spent hours in front of mirrors practicing control of facial expressions. A fleeting unconscious facial expression at the wrong time before the wrong person could result in death. Further, your Japanese teachers are not interested in your inner emotional states being advertised during practice. All of that is to be decorously hidden. You may be struggling. You may be confused. You may be afraid. Don't show it on your face. A good rule of thumb is found in the samurai saying, "Fire in the heart, ashes in the eyes."

Generally, Japanese find Westerners to be overly verbose, a tendency they associate with bores and children. I noticed that when I was being introduced at various academic gatherings my self-introduction was very different from that of my Japanese colleagues. As a Westerner, I introduced myself with a strong voice, erect posture, and direct eye contact. But my Japanese colleagues, when asked to introduce themselves, would often mumble something incoherent and stare at the floor as if they were deeply embarrassed, during which time audience members would chat with their neighbors or rise and move about the room. My American upbringing had taught me to "stand up tall" and "speak out," whereas the Japanese lesson was more along the lines of "the nail that sticks up is the nail you knock down." While I was sticking up all over the place, my Japanese colleagues were making themselves as inconspicuous as one possibly could while standing in front of a roomful of university personnel with a microphone in hand.

Use your eyes delicately and consciously. Do not stare into a person's eyes; this is seen as an aggressive signal anywhere in the world. Particularly when being communicated to by teachers or seniors, do not look into their eyes although they will be looking at yours. I learned to focus my eyes somewhere about throat level and watch the overall motion of the teacher with peripheral vision. Again, be ready for local custom, which might enjoin you to look at a spot on the sensei's forehead or, as in jodo, in the eye.

Gross body positioning, particularly in the martial arts, carries much information. I do not mean in this instance the subtle shoulder shrug or meaningful tilt of the head, but rather the large issues, such as where and how to stand under various circumstances. Where you position yourself vis-a-vis another speaks volumes. Because I am very tall by Japanese standards, and felt that towering over my teachers was somehow not respectful, I took pains to maintain as low a body posture as was practically possible while keeping within the standards of correct posture and balance.

In addition I would stand or position my body slightly to the left of a teacher under informal conditions. The communication here states that I am not attempting to stand in the way of the teacher's free movement and that I am putting the teacher in the position of seniority, that is, to my right. Do not, however, become so focused on proper standing and body positioning that your movements appear stiff and unnatural. Proper eye focusing and body positioning with relationship to teachers or seniors should be performed as naturally as possible. When in doubt, be polite by your own cultural standards. You will not be expected to know all the subtleties of wordless communication, sometimes called the "belly arts," because you have not been reared in Japanese culture. A sincere attempt to act politely will be understood, even if it is not precisely how a traditional Japanese *budoka* might act. Remember that the Japanese have been observing Westerners for hundreds of years and they probably understand Western forms of etiquette a lot better than Westerners know Japanese forms of etiquette. The issue of etiquette is of great importance. It is often said that budo begins and ends with courtesy.

Also, be very aware of your feet in a traditional dojo. They are vehicles of dirt carried into the dojo from the outside—"inside and outside" and "dirt and cleanliness" being very important polar relations in much of Japanese culture. Never sit with your feet facing the teacher or the dojo *kamiza*. Never sit in the dojo in any fashion that exposes your feet to view, and if you have to, be aware to hide your feet as efficiently as possible. Again, do not become obsessed with this, but rather try to work it into your everyday behavior while in Japan. Never leave socks lying in sight. Never wear your shoes in the dojo. Always have a pair of *zori* (sandals) just for dojo use and always be sure that your feet are clean and your nails trimmed before entering the dojo. With these customs in mind it can be seen that kicking a man carries with it more than merely a martial signal. To place your feet on another is profoundly insulting.

Brevity of expression is prized in Japan. In a martial arts setting speak not at all unless addressed by a teacher and then respond with as few words as possible. Japanese art is notoriously minimalist. Do more with less. When possible use body and hand gestures to communicate to your teacher during class. If you have to leave the practice area for some reason, a long verbal excuse is not required or even seemly. Rather, bow slightly to the teacher and raise one hand edge forward held at heart level. This gesture says, "May I be excused?" The teacher's response will likewise be minimal and nonverbal—a slight nod, a brief wave of the hand, or flick of the fingers.

Do not despair of ever having the opportunity to speak freely with your teachers. All dojo have a social life (parties and group restaurant or bar outings) in which a more informal air predominates. Under those conditions talk all you like. However, remember that the level of familiarity that may be tolerated while drinking and partying is not to be carried over into formal dojo practice. The strict rules of the dojo are ancient, and have a purpose which becomes increasingly clear as your years of training increase.

If you lack Japanese verbal skills, you may wonder how you will fare in a Japanese dojo. You have several things going for you. First, verbal exchange has very little to do with the teaching of most Japanese arts. The teachers teach and demonstrate while the students pay attention. In the traditional dojo, students never comment or ask questions while the teacher is demonstrating. Even at the university level I found that one of the major differences between Japanese and American college students was that the American students were encouraged to raise their hands, ask questions, challenge the teacher's statements, and verbally spar with the professors. This is called "classroom participation." However, such behavior in Japanese educational institutions would be highly improper. In informal conversations with Japanese college students I probed to understand why they would not raise their hands in class and ask questions. The general thrust was that to do so was to assume that the teacher lacked the skill to anticipate every question that a lowly student could generate. The assumption is that the teacher will teach all that is needed when the time is right.

The characteristic lack of verbal exchange between student and teacher in traditional Japanese martial arts training also proved to be a way in which I understood that I was "connecting" with my Japanese classmates in the practice of Muso-ryu jodo at the Fukuoka Budokan. One evening the British Olympic Judo team, which had been practicing at the budokan, sat in with the jodo class to experience another Japanese martial art. As the teacher was demonstrating a particular sword and short-staff set, one of the judo players, a very nice young man it turns out, raised his hand and shouted out a question in a loud booming voice. I could feel the ripple of tension run through my fellow jodo students as we sat shoulder to shoulder in line facing the teacher. I even found myself sucking air through my teeth with a soft hiss in a typical Japanese gesture of discomfort. At that moment I felt what my Japanese college students might experience if I had insisted that they speak to me during my classes at the university. I never brought up the issue with them again.

On the way home from the budokan that night, as I walked through the grounds of the nearby Zen garden, I remember thinking how quickly dojo bonding can happen. I had automatically reacted in a Japanese fashion to the behavior of Westerners, people who were culturally and historically my people, after only about five months in a Japanese *jodojo*. This example also suggests that a deep, almost unconscious bonding with dojo mates can happen across cultural and linguistic barriers, even when the language skills are lacking on both sides. The Japanese martial arts, like all arts, are a universal language. If you don't actively attempt to impede their work, they will reveal their inner form in time.

If there is one act that sums up practically everything I've touched upon in this chapter (etiquette, sensitivity, correct behavior), it is the bow. The first thing you do and the last thing you do in a Japanese martial arts class is to bow. Obviously that act must be very important.

It should be remembered that bowing is also found in the West. Proper bowing, in Europe and the United Kingdom, was an art of nobility. Of Westerners, Americans would claim that they bow to no one because they are a people who have never acknowledged kings nor existed as a feudal society. This is sometimes a problem when

Western students enter a school or dojo teaching Japanese martial arts. But Americans do bow. We bow to the applause of others. We bow before religious leaders. When someone gives us a present we proffer a slight dip of the head. We bow our head in defeat. In fact, the next time you are observing close friends greeting one another, observe the angle of the neck, head, and upper back. At some point during the exchange of greetings each individual will tilt his or her upper body axis in the direction of each of the others. You might liken the Japanese bow to the Western custom of shaking hands. When Western men greet one another and extend their right hands in greeting the precise nature of that simple gesture can express a wide range of information about the relationship of the two men. You can watch men shake hands and usually tell whether it is a greeting of equals or an exchange between two men of markedly different status. The lower status male bows slightly as he shakes hands with his superior who does not bow. A handshake can also communicate warmth, aloofness, eagerness, anger, affection, threat, and sincerity. For a Westerner going to Japan not to take cognizance of bowing would be like a Japanese businessman taking his first trip to New York without being aware of the intricacies of American hand-shaking customs.

It was fascinating to observe, and attempt to take part in, the many contexts and intricacies of bowing. There was a gas station on the corner about a block from our house. When a customer drove in, a friendly full-service crew would quickly wash the windows, pump the gasoline, check the oil and tires, and send them on their way. It was the last part that was most fun to watch. After pumping the customer's gas the crew would stop the traffic on the street allowing the freshly serviced customer to exit, who as he drove away he would see in his rearview mirror the entire crew bowing to him from the waist, their backs at a forty-five degree angle. My Japanese colleagues jokingly told me that after a hard day's work they sometimes went to such service stations to get "energy and respect."

Once, as we were leaving a restaurant after a formal dinner given for my family and me, I noticed that my four Japanese colleagues were not with us. I walked back toward the dining room area and saw them standing in the hallway outside the room in which we had eaten, bowing to one another. If I could have taken a picture of them at that moment the precise angle of their bows would have allowed me to rank them in terms of prestige and status. The act can be that precise.

One of the most powerful martial arts experiences I had while in Japan came in the form of a bow. One morning I had gone to the *kyu-dojo* early to practice before the test I was about to take. When I arrived, seeing no one, I went into the locker room to change. I stayed in the locker room for awhile after changing, testing the dojo's bows. During that time another *kyudoka* arrived, changed, and was on the shooting floor with her bow and arrows when I came out of the locker room. When I saw her I froze in embarrassment because I recognized her as one of my archery teacher's friends, another kyudo master (*hanshi*). With full composure, the woman turned toward me and, with bow and arrows in hand, performed a sitting bow with such control and dignity that I felt as if a power were emanating from her and pushing me back. I was very well aware that while she was in the process of bowing I could not move forward. You may wonder why a master would bother showing such behavior to me, a nobody, a white belt. I wondered too, but I was grateful to her for allowing me to experience the kind of politeness that the samurai called "power in repose."

My kyudo sensei used bowing in a similar manner. When her students arrived at the dojo for practice, she would greet them with a deep bow, sometimes exceeding a forty-five degree angle. Her students would often spontaneously attempt to bow lower in order to show proper respect. Since she only came up to my chest, my attempt to return her deep bow was ludicrous in the extreme. I solved the problem by focusing on projecting the feeling of a dignified bow to my archery sensei since I knew I had lost the low bow battle. When all else fails, seek to project the most sincere spirit you can muster. The importance of the proper bow has even generated computer software that can train one for the perfect bow by using feedback signals. If the central axis of the bower's body does not perfectly match the angle projected by the computer, a light flashes or a buzzer sounds.

The standing bow (*ritsurei*) should be executed whenever entering or leaving the dojo precincts, when greeted or addressed by dojo mates and teachers (the exact dip of the bow indicating relative rank, but don't become obsessed with this in the beginning), at various times during practice when working with partners, and when it is announced that a senior personage has entered the dojo.

There are many variations on exactly how to angle the feet for this bow. Study the foot placement of the seniors to learn the particular custom of your dojo. Until you can figure that out, it would be acceptable to stand with your feet a few inches apart at the heels and the front of your feet angled slightly to the outside. The stance should communicate ease and stability. Keeping your spine and the back of your head in alignment, bow from the waist with the knees locked (it is not a curtsy). Hold the position for a few beats and realign your body. Do not bend your head forward as you bow. This would present a view of the nape of your neck to someone to whom you were bowing, a definite faux pas. While bowing place your hands, if you are male, palms inward aligned down the outside of your thighs. If female, place the hands on the front of the thighs at the deepest part of your bow. But, as with all aspects of custom, watch carefully exactly how your dojo mates perform this common bow. In some places both men and women may place their hands on the front of their thighs while bowing.

The seated bow (*zarei*) is performed from the formal sitting position (*seiza*). First, step back with the left foot and kneel, bringing the right foot into a kneeling position as you slowly sit on your ankles. Your feet should be splayed in a "V" shape under you. Keeping the head and the back erect, place your hands palm downward on your thighs. To bow, tilt your body forward, buttocks not lifting from ankles, head and back not losing alignment. Bow from the waist at a thirty-degree angle to the floor as you place your hands, left hand first, in a triangular shape, fingers tight together, thumbs extended, to about six inches in front of your knees. The effect is that you are looking into the center of a triangle formed by your hands. Hold the bow for a few beats and then realign the body, lifting first the right hand and then the left.

There are many "hidden" features in the Japanese martial arts. Discovering them through time is part of the enjoyment of any art.

For example, the fact that in *zarei* the student first steps back with the left foot and kneels before withdrawing the right foot is in homage to the swordsmen, who carried the sword on their left hip, and whose priority in sitting and standing was the ability to draw the sword quickly. In similar vein, when you place your left hand on the floor first, it is acknowledging that the right hand, the sword-drawing hand, is still free. Likewise, when rising from the seated bow, the first hand you release from the floor is the sword-drawing hand. And finally, when rising from *zarei*, the student advances the right foot first, again the more comfortable position for rapid sword-drawing. In some dojo, after bringing the left foot into position next to the right, the bower then steps back to cancel the aggressive advance of the first rising movement out of *zarei*.

Don't become intimidated by the complexity and difficulty of Japanese bowing customs. Ueshiba Morihei, when asked about the proper method of bowing, said that the most important thing is the sincerity of the spirit of the one bowing. Note, however, that Ueshiba Sensei is suggesting that he can discern your spirit by your bow. This is always assumed. So follow written instructions on bowing, which can be found in dozens of books on Japanese culture, watch local custom closely, and practice the great central goal of all Japanese martial arts: expressing your mind/spirit/heart through your body.

Finally, though martial arts training sessions are fairly regularized, there is also what is called "special training," times when the pattern is broken, often by leaving the precincts of the dojo for training. I have found this phenomenon in every martial art I have practiced or researched. My karatedo sensei once showed us pictures of winter training in northern Japan. The *karatedoka* in the photos, dressed in their *dogi*, were up their knees in snow as they practiced basic *kihon waza*, *kata*, and *kumite*.

Beach training is also common. Running and practicing precise foot movement in sand will make you long for your dojo floor. You may find yourself waist deep in the surf, trying to maintain balance as you punch and kick against the incoming breakers. Or your sense of focus may be challenged by being asked to fish from the beach ... without bait or hook.

On New Year's Eve, an *aikidojo* may have "special training" in which the students cut with their *bokken* five hundred times to purify themselves, the dojo, and the coming year; while another dojo may wade into icy river waters up their chins to practice breathing exercises. The variations on "special training" are endless, but always challenging.

Life in a dojo in Japan becomes much simpler once you realize that most of what Japanese budoka do during class is to act like good Japanese citizens: full of enthusiasm, sincerity, team spirit, orderliness, respect, and peace whether they are sitting, standing, exercising, sparring, stretching, or performing basic punching, kicking, and blocking drills. If you time a Japanese budo class but count only the time when the students are actually involved with the physical techniques of the style they are practicing, you will find that the "doing nothing" (sitting, waiting, listening, etc.) part of the class is almost equal to the "doing technique" part of the class. The conclusion one would have to reach is that what is being practiced in a Japanese martial arts class is to a large extent the values and ideals of Japanese social culture, the goal of which is to achieve and maintain *wa*, or social harmony.

Testing for Rank in a Japanese Dojo

After about six months of regular training you may be asked to test for rank. You are not allowed to demur. That you test at a particular point is your teacher's decision, not yours. Testing is also part of budo training. It is always stressful and is supposed to be. Relax, wait patiently, and trust your teacher's judgement on matters of testing. It is generally assumed that if your teacher requests that you to test for rank, he or she is sure you are capable of passing such a test. During my time in Japan I was asked by the teachers of two of the arts I practiced, kyudo and jodo, to test for rank; first-degree brown belt (ikkyu) in the former instance and shodan (first-degree black belt) in the latter, after almost a year in training.

To move from beginner to first-degree black belt in one year is not at all typical in budo, but I was not a beginner when I went to Japan. I had twenty years of martial arts training under my belt, a *nidan* (second-degree black belt) rank in Sakugawa Koshiki Shorinji-ryu karatedo and *sandan* (third-degree black belt) in Ueshiba-ryu aikido. The lessons learned from karatedo and aikido training in the United States were automatically applied when I entered archery and staff-fighting dojo in Japan. Proper attitude toward teachers and seniors, knowledge of basic dojo etiquette, intense training attitude, consciousness of posture and stance, a constant awareness of respect for all things and all people around me, coupled with the study and practice of karatedo *kata* and the staff and sword of aikido separated me from the beginning Japanese student at the outset.

I was asked by Asakuma Shihan to test for *nikyu* (second-degree brown belt) at an upcoming examination which would draw together many of the kyudo master teachers of Kyushu and several hundred of their students. In preparation I focused on the basic shooting *kata* which involved shooting two arrows over a twenty-eight meter range at a target about fourteen inches in diameter. The arrows are custom made to fit the student. In my case I was shooting arrows that were forty-two inches long with a composite bamboo bow that stood over seven feet.

The basic shooting *kata* begin with very precisely ritualized steps used to enter the shooting area and approach to the shooting line, fit and raise the arrow, shoot, kneel to refit the second arrow, rise in posture, shoot again, and leave the shooting area. Each step is fixed by the traditional *kata* routine. I practiced almost six hours a week, and in each two-hour session I shot about thirty to forty arrows, hitting the target on an average of one to two times if I was having a good day.

The test was held in the town of Agi at the foot of an ancient castle. There were hundreds of Japanese archery students present. My wife and I were the only foreigners present. We were sent onto the shooting floor in groups of four. At a long table against the wall facing the shooters sat the judges' panel, composed of seven venerable old kyudo *shihan*. When my turn came to shoot I could see large groups of Japanese kyudo students move toward the fence on the side of the shooting range to see the tall *gaijin* (foreigner) shoot, a sight few of them had seen in that part of Japan. I was aware of them and also aware of the penetrating gaze of the *shihan* who sat about ten feet in front of me. However, as most martial artists know, *kata* training enables the student to enter a quiet and private space. I blocked out all the surrounding distractions as I lost myself in the breathing patterns and precise movements of my *kata*.

My first shot hit the center of the target. I wasn't aware at the time how important that hit was. I later found that no other student testing for upper *kyu* ranks that day had hit the target. I was the only one. My second shot came close but missed. I completed my *kata* and left the shooting area.

As my teachers and fellow students were congratulating me a senior student, a fifth-degree black belt who spoke some English, came up to me and asked me to follow him to the examination room. I had not heard of an "examination room" in my preparation for the day's testing. When I asked him what was to happen next he said, "You hit the target. You must now test for *shodan*." When I asked him what the *shodan* test would be, he said, "Now you must answer some questions."

The rank of *shodan* is awarded if the test panel judges that your *kata* is correct, showing "poignancy and internal *kiai*," as one *kyudoka* put it; if you hit the target, and if you pass a written test. The written examination that awaited me consisted of three questions. The first asked me to recount the history of kyudo, the second question directed me to select one of the postures in the shooting *kata* and to describe it in detail, while the third question required an essay describing the goals of budo training. I was prepared for this test because I had misunderstood earlier instructions and thought that these questions would be asked of me for advancement to the rank of *nikyu*. Therefore, I had studied for the test. Furthermore, reading on the nature, history, and philosophy of the martial arts as well as excellent preparation in the United States under Cauley Shihan, United States director of Sakugawa Koshiki Shorinji-ryu karatedo, and Saotome Shihan of Ueshiba-ryu aikido, plus lengthy discussions with seniors and fellow budoka in the United States enabled me to tell the Japanese archery teachers what they wanted to hear concerning the spiritual nature of budo training and its goal of creating the citizens of a peaceful society. Several Japanese students did not pass to *shodan* rank because in their written test they had described the goal of budo training as the creation of physical strength, toughness, and fighting ability, a type of response that one budo sensei described as "unseasoned and immature."

I learned an important lesson that day when I returned from my successful written test and was told that I had been promoted to *shodan*. When Asakuma Shihan congratulated me, I said, "I was just lucky." I was! There were days at the *kyudojo* when I shot forty times and never came close to hitting the target. However, when my comments were translated to Asakuma Shihan, she frowned at me and the tone of her comments told me I was being scolded for something. The senior student translated. She was telling me that saying I was merely lucky was an insult to her teaching! I had hit the target because of her training! I had hit the target because it was my karma to hit the target at that place and at that time! I was there for a reason! There is no luck! I was reminded of the old Zen saying, "A snowflake does not fall in the wrong place."

My experience testing for *shodan* in Muso-ryu jodo shared some of the qualities of my kyudo testing with some added elements. Testing for *shodan* is possible when the student has "mastered" the basic techniques of the *jo* as well as the twelve *seitei kata* (standard fighting forms). The *kata* begin with simple forms involving only two or three techniques, and advance by graded steps to the twelfth in the series, which involves about thirty techniques. The *kata* are named Tsuki Zue (Standing Stick), Suigetsu (Moon in the Water), Ran Ai (Harmony Out of Chaos), and so on.

As with kyudo, the jodo testing situation involved several hundred students from all over the Kyushu area. It was held in the Fukuoka Budokan. The jodo *shihan* sat behind a long table with Otofuji Shihan, the headmaster of the style. Before the examination, Otofuji Shihan, elderly and barely able to walk, addressed the students lined up for the test and stressed the importance of "sincere effort," "brightness of spirit," "manly behavior," and "citizenship" as the "heart of jodo."

The *shodan* test allowed the students to select five of the *seitei kata* to perform before the panel of *shihan*, although we were not told this until minutes before our names were called to approach the testing area. A similar pattern of testing is reported by Michael Finn in his interesting account of training in iaido in Japan, *Iaido: The Way of The Sword* (1982:13). He writes:

> Soon the day of my examination came. I was absolutely amazed when Kuroda Sensei (after all the training I had done) told me I could choose any four kata out of the twelve studied to do for the exam. I

had expected far worse. At the hall, there were many young Japanese taking the same exam as myself; perhaps about two hundred.

Fortunately, in my jodo exam I had the assistance of Ogata Sensei, a seventh-*dan*, who played the part of the swordsman, while I was to defend with the short staff. I appreciated the old samurai maxim that one should be grateful for an excellent opponent. Ogata Sensei's spirited and precise sword attacks made my job easier.

We went onto the budokan floor in sets of four as several hundred jodo students watched. In turn, we called out the name of our *kata* and proceeded with our demonstration. I started with the third most difficult *kata*, just to see how I would do with Ogata Sensei as a partner. When I became aware that his expertise was making me look good, I called out the top four most difficult *kata* to complete my remaining requirements for testing. Again, as with kyudo, my testing attracted a crowd of spectators, but after almost a year practicing in Fukuoka I had become used to drawing crowds at such events.

When I left the testing area I immediately approached Ogata Sensei, bowed deeply and thanked him for his assistance. He slapped me on the shoulder and said, "No problem." Next I was directed to a far corner of the budokan where the written portion of the test was taking place. The format was the same as for the kyudo *shodan* written test. I was asked to discuss the history of Shinto Muso-ryu jodo, describe one of the *seitei kata* in detail, and conclude with an essay on the merits of jodo training. Again, the "right" answers had to do with what Otofuji Shihan had said in his comments at the beginning of the testing session about citizenship, brightness of spirit, and sincere effort; a "wrong" answer stressed the acquisition of physical strength and fighting ability. It should be noted, of course, that strength, courage, and combat ability are rightly considered high priorities of budo training, but they are never considered the most important goals to seek. They come as automatic accompaniment to training carried out at more lofty levels of consciousness, and it is that higher level that budo sensei want to hear about, and even more important, to see reflected in behavior.

It intrigued me to discover that, in the case of many of the Japanese jodo students, as with some of the kyudo students, the point of budo training was totally misunderstood. Most of the beginner Japanese budo students apparently do not read books on the subject, and only rarely, as in the case of Otofugi Shihan's address to the testing jodo students, do budo sensei explain the essential point of budo training to them. I found myself in the somewhat embarrassing situation of being promoted to *shodan* in jodo while better physical specimens than I were held back. The only difference was that I had the "right" responses to the written portion of the *shodan* test. Japanese budo sensei place great stress on the mature thought processes and civilized behavior of their advanced students.

I feel very grateful for the opportunity I had to train and test for rank in Japanese dojo and to experience first hand teaching of *hanshi-* level teachers of the martial way. I learned many physical techniques from my teachers and had many penetrating insights into my own psyche and nature. I found that my formative training in the deeper meanings of budo, coming from instructors in America—notably Cauley Shihan and Saotome Shihan—was what separated me from the other "beginner" students in the two dojo in which I trained. The teachers in the United States who had created the foundation of my understanding of budo enabled me to find success in Japan, and to them I am very, very grateful.

(This chapter first appeared as an article "Testing for Shodan in Japan: Kyudo and Jyodo," in *Journal of Asian Martial Arts*, Vol. 1, No. 1, January 1992, and is used by permission.)

Twenty-First-Century Samurai:
An Interview with Mitsugi Saotome Shihan

The following interview was conducted on September 12, 1999, at the home of Mitsugi Saotome Shihan, headmaster of the Aikido Schools of Ueshiba. Saotome Sensei was uchi deshi (inner student) to the founder of aikido, Ueshiba Morihei, and instructor of instructors at the Aikikai Hombu Dojo in Tokyo for many years. He has written several books on aikido and travels the world giving seminars. I thought it might be useful to acquire the perspective of a Japanese martial arts teacher concerning the presence of Westerners training in Japanese dojo. I have included a transcription of the entire interview to show that a budo sensei ranges far and wide in his thinking and that most of his response is related to the necessity for clear thought, education, and sensitivity.

JONES: What advice would you give to a Westerner who wished to go to Japan to study Japanese martial arts?

SAOTOME SENSEI: Japanese culture is very old, thousands of years. It is a very complicated society, more than many other societies. On very small islands. People live so compact. So for Western people who go there for learning something, you must ask "What is my purpose?" You must focus your intent. You must have a clear purpose in mind. A clear focus. The reason is that each Japanese area—Kyushu, Osaka, Kyoto—is so different. Japan is a complex traditional society in many, many ways.

JONES: What could you tell Westerners about training in Japan that would help them maintain their focus, help keep them from making mistakes?

SAOTOME SENSEI: People go to study in Japan for many different reasons. Some people go to study Japanese martial art. They may be looking for authority. Many martial arts students go to Japan and study. They come back to the United States and say, "Oh, I have studied in Japan for many years. I am an authority because I have studied in Japan." But what kind of skill do they have? It is not important where the skill came from. What kind of teachers did they have? Do they have a feeling for serious learning?

JONES: How can a Westerner know if the Japanese teacher is truly skilled?

SAOTOME SENSEI: This is a problem. But I think that the starting point is "What is your reason for going to Japan?" One says, "I'm going to study serious Japanese martial art." One says, "I'm going to be a playboy." It is all about individual attitude. I don't believe that many Westerners go there to study with serious attitude. I have a lot of experience with Westerners in Japan. I have seen many students come to Tokyo Hombu. Some are really weird people.

JONES: Weird? Are you talking about different motives? Different reasons for study?

SAOTOME SENSEI: Oh, yes!

JONES: In your experience, what wrong things did Western students look for in martial arts training in Japan?

SAOTOME SENSEI: How many people do I see being serious? People who come every day for training at the dojo? At Hombu Dojo I see people come one day a week and later they say, "Oh, I have studied in Japan." Nothing! Not serious! Other times . . . where do they go? Being playboy, maybe. They are not serious. Looking for woman, maybe. But some people are very serious. Everybody has different reasons for going to Japan to study martial arts.

JONES: What is the best reason?

SAOTOME SENSEI: To be serious. Every day, you should go to the dojo for training. Don't be a playboy. I see so many spoiled people. Americans, or French, or Japanese ... many spoiled people. They come to the dojo only one day a week, or one day a month. Just use it as an excuse to stay in Japan. "Oh, I am student of Japanese art," they say. Or they looking for certificate to take home. But I only see them a day or two. At other times, where do they go? Go to be Western playboy, maybe. How many people are serious? Some people are very directed, but not everybody.

JONES: Will a Japanese budo sensei pay any attention to a Western beginner?

SAOTOME SENSEI: It depends. It is personal. I, for many years, take care of students at Hombu. But I do not pay attention to playboy ... those with no serious attitude. They come to Japan, teach English, teach French. They're not serious in their training for martial arts. They are looking to find a party all the time. They take easy life. You must work! Nobody cares that you are studying something Japanese. Japanese already know it, or don't care.

JONES: If a Westerner manages to join a dojo, what must he or she do to behave correctly?

SAOTOME SENSEI: It depends, but it is important that it is personal. And it's not just about Americans. Not just about French, or outside people. The person comes as student. The person. Not American. Not Japanese. Not French. The person. Also, Japanese budo teacher is watching all the time. I watch for the quality of a human being, not American or Japanese. Human being.

JONES: So you would say that if a Western student enters a Japanese martial arts class, he or she can count on being observed closely?

SAOTOME SENSEI: Oh, yes! A sensei will watch carefully. A student might not know it.

JONES: What would you advise a Westerner about dojo etiquette? About bowing?

SAOTOME SENSEI: It is not a Westerner's problem. It is a people problem. You should show respect. Some say, "I'm an American, I don't care." But some Japanese students don't care. It is about the individual. Some students are very sincere. Some show no respect. This is not about nation. It is about individual personal character. Show your respect. Show your intelligence. Show that you respect yourself. You must be serious. You must be sincere to learn. I don't think about Western and Eastern. In the long run, it is about the individual, not their nation.

JONES: So you don't think that talking about West and East has any use?

SAOTOME SENSEI: No. You live and die as *you* . . . not as French, or American, or Japanese.

JONES: So both Japanese and American students, for example, would make the same kind of mistakes?

SAOTOME SENSEI: Yes. I don't like arrogant students. Insulting students. Students with too much pride. Personal behavior. Not East and West. Some Americans might say, "I'm from Texas. I'm a cowboy." It doesn't matter. Everybody is individual. A Japanese budo sensei doesn't care if you are a cowboy, or French. You are a student. Are you a good student? Are you an arrogant student? Are you sincere? Are you serious? For many, many years in Japan, I see many, many American students.

JONES: So it is possible that a Western student may be a better martial arts student than a Japanese student?

SAOTOME SENSEI: Oh, yes! Student must be very sincere for learning. That's all. Not Eastern . . . Western. No, I don't think so. It is all about a personal quality. You have it? You don't have it? You want it? It is also about education. When an educated person comes to training, they will study. They know how to study. They know how to show respect. But then some times, punk kind of people come. Japanese punk comes. American punk comes. It doesn't matter. Punks never learn anything no matter what their nation is.

JONES: So Western students should think about sincere attitude, showing respect, being humble . . . .

SAOTOME SENSEI: Yes! Humble . . . good virtue.

JONES: What are some of the kinds of mistakes that Westerners make when they come to Japan to train?

SAOTOME SENSEI: Not mistakes. It is very difficult to learn structure of another culture. Need some time to understand where you are. Student needs some neutral time to adapt to new environment. It takes adjusting time. Japanese know that. A Japanese budo sensei knows that. Just living in Japan is confusing to new person. Where to buy food? Where do you stay? How do you get to dojo? Before going to Japan, you must do a lot of research on Japanese society, history—you need to become an intelligent person. It's no good if you go to Japan and have no idea of history of Japanese people. Why do they do that? Why do they do this? Study before you come to Japan. Level of education is important to what can be learned in new experience. When a Japanese person goes to America, goes to Europe—same thing. In any society people should respect education and what is behind education—sincere work, training. I saw that students with good educational background were more serious in training.

JONES: When I was in Japan, I saw many types of dojos, but there was one that I really didn't understand. Some were for college students. Some were for families, but some seemed to have only young Japanese men who were very muscled and who usually had their hair cut short. These people did not like foreigners or women to train with them. Who are they?

SAOTOME SENSEI: Some kind of antisocial people—maybe gangsters. Martial art gangsters. This kind of mentality doesn't care if they hurt people. Like some motorcycle gangs. These kind of people are very close to social outcast—mean spirited. But every society has people like that. Not just in martial arts. They are very isolated— gangsters. Some look to me like Japanese red-neck. Maybe Japanese nationalistic people don't like any other people. But there are all kinds of different groups and all kinds of different dojo.

JONES: If a Westerner goes to some town on Shikoku, for example, and wants to find a dojo to practice in, but they can't speak Japanese or read Japanese, what should they do?

SAOTOME SENSEI: This is a very difficult question. There are certain kinds of associations and organizations to help Westerners find martial art study. Go to a budokan. Almost all towns have them. They might have library too, maybe offices. Some budokan are national, some are local. They are administrative centers for budo. I think most budokan are supported by local government.

JONES: Am I right to think that the martial arts teachers at the budokans are of a very high caliber?

SAOTOME SENSEI: Yes, I think so. Go to budokan. Don't go to gangster dojo. I am being serious! Be very careful! Some Japanese people hate *gaijin* (foreigners). Some people very narrow. People in any country have same kinds of groups.

JONES: You have said that a serious purpose of training is necessary. How can a Westerner who doesn't speak Japanese explain their purpose?

SAOTOME SENSEI: Don't need to explain. Need to show. Also, it is good to have a letter from some teacher to say you are serious student. Letters are important. I give you letter and you go to Hombu and everybody take care of you. You don't speak Japanese—doesn't matter. You are my student. Students who go to Japan with my recommendation have no problems. Never have problems.

JONES: If I am going to Japan to train and I am a black belt, should I wear my black belt or should I wear a white belt?

SAOTOME SENSEI: Some would say to wear white belt. Some would say to wear black belt. I don't care. A belt is a belt. Some black belts act like white belts and some white belts act better than black belts. Watch for local customs—different parts of Japan have different customs about such things.

JONES: What about *dogi* with club patches and flag sewn on them? Should a Westerner wear such a decorated *dogi* in Japan?

SAOTOME SENSEI: No problem for me. Everything you do shows who you are. What do you think? Japanese dojo have patches that show where they come from. Use judgment. Is it respectful?

In Japan it is very important who your teacher is. You have black belt in such and such an organization, what does black belt mean? Depends on who your teacher is.

JONES: If a Westerner is going to Japan to study martial arts, and he doesn't speak Japanese, are there any phrases that you suggest they learn in order to communicate with their Japanese teachers or seniors?

SAOTOME SENSEI: If you go anywhere, study basic language of people who live there. Westerners say, "Oh, I go to Japan and everybody speaks English." No. Also learn polite language. Most important to say "Thank you," say "Excuse me," or "Hello." To show respect. To show gratitude. Sometimes Americans are different. Some Americans think the whole world speaks English. Americans often go to some other country and ask, "Do you speak English?" Other people from other countries are not so pushy in this way. Americans—West to East Coast—all speak same language. But outside of America, how many people speak English? But only Americans push and say, "Hey, do you speak English?" This is very arrogant. Do you think so?

JONES: I never thought about it that way.

SAOTOME SENSEI: If I go to France, I say, "Excuse me, I cannot speak French." I don't say, "Do you speak Japanese?" Do you see the difference? English is not official language in the world. Be careful that you are not arrogant. From one culture to another, you must be a diplomat.

JONES: It sounds like you are saying that Westerners, if they don't learn Japanese customs at least a little, come off appearing to be arrogant or disrespectful?

SAOTOME SENSEI: Yeah. I think so. How many people come from some other place to America and say, "Do you speak French?" No. It is a little thing, maybe, but little things are important. American people are most likely to say, "Do you speak English?"

JONES: Why do you think that is?

SAOTOME SENSEI: I don't know. American people may not be so sensitive about ... they don't usually have other people to talk to. All over the country they speak English. Big surprise when they don't. This is not just about language. It is about communication. Martial arts has a lot to do with communication. Pushing is not good. Yes, America is very great country. Everybody respect. No need to push.

JONES: On a different subject, how should a Westerner training in Japan respond to Japanese bullies in the dojo?

SAOTOME SENSEI: This is a very difficult question. Sometimes it is misunderstanding. In American society, everybody flat, equal. Outside in society, everybody is equal. That is fine. But in Japan traditional culture is very structured: sensei, *sempai, kohai* . . .

American people have difficulty learning this. Who is above? Who is below? Teacher-student position—very different. Make sure. Maybe not bully. Maybe *sempai*. But I understand "bully." Cowards. I don't need them in my dojo.

Also, America and Europe very different. They are not both same as Westerners. European people better understand martial arts than American, because European society has class-consciousness. Kings. Knights. America and Europe are completely different—to me as a Japanese man. Most Americans don't understand that positions in society can be very different. Americans find it hard to follow authority guidelines. Always protest. They say, "Oh, sensei teaches this way, but my ideas are different." Europeans not so much protesting. Do you understand? I think it is easier for a European student to go to Japan and understand than for Americans. Most hard for Americans. A lot of American students have cowboy attitude.

JONES: Is that a standard prejudice . . . .

SAOTOME SENSEI: No prejudice . . . .

JONES: To say that Americans are cowboys . . . .

SAOTOME SENSEI: I don't think so.

JONES: That's not prejudice . . . .

SAOTOME SENSEI: Not prejudice. Japanese look at Western student— American, Australian, European—all the same in reality. But American student attitude often shows them to be cowboys.

JONES: What about when you teach in South America? Are they more like Americans or Europeans?

SAOTOME SENSEI: Europeans! I feel they have a traditional . . . a more structured society than in America. America is only two hundred years. It has a constitution. Everybody equal. That is very hard to understand in other countries. No *sempai-kohai* ranking system. No tradition. Americans have little tradition of social classes which make this kind of ranking system accepted in society. Very hard. South American still has European influence—Spanish, Portuguese, German, they are all there.

JONES: Will American culture ever be able to sustain its own martial art tradition without the ideas of social ranking found in Japan?

SAOTOME SENSEI: This is a very hard question. This is what I am looking for. This is a paradox. American people hate equality.

JONES: What?

SAOTOME SENSEI: Everybody says, "I am different than the other one." But the United States Constitution says, "Everybody, all the time is equal." But American people seem to hate equality. This is paradox in consciousness. "I'm unique. I'm different than the other." This is very American mentality in my experience.

JONES: Don't Japanese individuals feel that they are unique?

SAOTOME SENSEI: Yeah. Japanese people as individuals are very unique people—individually. But they value cooperation and harmony. Both.

JONES: Americans have the same basic idea, don't they?

SAOTOME SENSEI: I don't think so. American people hate equality. This is where there is a big screw-up. Be unique—like criminal population. What behavior is best? Be unique or be equal? America is most organized society in the world. They've got to be, because of paradox. Outlaw attitude. Cowboy attitude. Fantasy. But where is the organization? You see? They say, "I'm outlaw. I have freedom."

JONES: But from Japan, Westerners see "samurai movies" where the lone swordsman stands alone. This is like old-time ideas of cowboy gunfighters in the Old West.

SAOTOME SENSEI: Yes. Samurai is very close to American ideas. That's why Americans like samurai movies, *yakuza* movies.

JONES: The lone samurai image in Japan seems . . .

SAOTOME SENSEI: Not alone. They are acting for society. Motive is for society, justice, order. The most organized society—Japan and America. They both like some kind of outlaw, but Japanese *yakuza* are most organized of all of Japanese society. Outlaws! Gangs often have very strict laws. It is another paradox? In America you have Jesse James—outlaw. American people love some kind of outlaws. Japan too. But outlaw is hero to young people, not for mature people. Fantasy. You go join a gang. You have no freedom. You must wear this kind of shirt, and this kind of hair, and this kind of colors. No freedom, even for outlaw—especially for outlaw. A lot of martial arts students are fantasy outlaws. Young people, not mature people. Playing outlaw. They want to be free. Not possible. I don't care about organization, but I need organization. You want freedom. How can you have freedom? If you have freedom, who protects your freedom? United States government. You are an American and you say, "I have my freedom." I don't think so. Is everybody free to kill you? No. A lot of people misunderstand this. Are you free to travel anywhere in the world? No, if you lose your passport. Are you free? You can be free in another country, if you don't break other country's law. Are you all the way free? Who is behind your freedom?

JONES: Do people have freedom in the martial arts in Japan? In a particular style, is there freedom?

SAOTOME SENSEI: In natural training style, freedom is limited. You cannot fly in the sky. You cannot breathe under water. In studying freedom you must understand unfreedom. American people think of freedom in a fantasy of reality.

JONES: In terms of ranking in the Japanese martial arts, is there a time in such a system when a person is supposed to become free to create?

SAOTOME SENSEI: Cannot be free! Ranking is never about freedom. It is about responsibility. If you have no capacity, no ability—what are you free from?

JONES: Should a student in budo accept that he will never be free?

SAOTOME SENSEI: What is freedom? You are an intelligent person— but what is freedom? Freedom has another side, which is about limitations. The physical is limited. Your biology is limited.

JONES: So you want me to accept that there is no freedom?

SAOTOME SENSEI: There is no freedom! Truly free people understand that there is no freedom. Freedom is to have a compass.

JONES: But in a particular society you might find a slave. He is totally unfree. But are all the people in that society like the slave?

SAOTOME SENSEI: Everybody not free is some kind of slave.

JONES: But you said . . . .

SAOTOME SENSEI: Jones! Are you free? You want to fly like a bird? Go ahead. You are free to try. Freedom understands that the physical is limited—maybe not the mental.

JONES: Is a person who has experienced *satori* [enlightenment] free?

SAOTOME SENSEI: Is my freedom in space or time? Unfreedom knowledge and freedom knowledge is the same.

JONES: So even the Buddha is not free?

SAOTOME SENSEI: No freedom. People who have experienced *satori* best understand that there is no freedom. Everything has to connect to everything else. Knowing that and living that is freedom.

JONES: Why are Americans so interested in the concept of freedom? For Americans, this is a major way that we define ourselves. We like to think we are free people.

SAOTOME SENSEI: What freedom? Fantasy. It is not just political rules. Such rules are not biological, not physical. Your law says you are free. True. If you are free, really free, rob a bank. Kill me. Fly like a bird while you flap your arms. Are you free? If you want to say you are—though it is really not important—you say you are free within limitations that you are not free of.

JONES: But a warrior in combat has got to be free . . . .

SAOTOME SENSEI: No! Warrior in battle must not be in a fantasy! This is very important to understand. Freedom and limitations are the same thing. Not different. You don't get to pick and choose. You cannot fly like a bird. You cannot dive like a whale. All warrior societies—Apache, Arab—all warrior societies understand that there is no freedom. Fighting the enemy looks like freedom, but it is not so inside you, not so in fact. If I push you, but overextend, I'm not free from what will then happen to me.

JONES: So budo sensei should teach freedom and limitations as part of the same thing . . .

SAOTOME SENSEI: Yes. This is military philosophy. This is military education.

JONES: What would be some other real basic aspects of military law?

SAOTOME SENSEI: Don't kill your own kind. Martial art may teach how to kill enemy, but enemy is enemy of home people. Never kill home people. This is a biological law with all creatures: never kill your own people. All military law in budo is biological. Extension of biological law. This is *bushido*. All is about protection of home people.

JONES: When does this biological behavior become spiritual?

SAOTOME SENSEI: It is spiritual! Military law is biological. When you act in terms of nature's law, God's law, you are acting spiritually. Budo is extension of natural law. It would not be real if it were not—it would not have meaning. People talk about races—white, yellow, red, black—but all are the same people. To see the same truth in what appears to be difference is interesting.

JONES: In what ways are budo sensei . . .

SAOTOME SENSEI: Budo sensei are not really important people. Maybe they are expert in martial art. But compared to doctor who works to save life every day, or compared to scientists who find new foods for starving people—martial arts teacher only being martial arts teacher is not very important. That is not what you want to try to be. Crushing other people because you are stronger or have more knowledge of martial arts technique—don't be proud of that. I'm not proud of that. I don't respect Musashi. He is a good killer. Many Japanese respect Musashi. I don't respect. People might think of me breaking other peoples bones—but what kind of spiritual life do I have? I would be ashamed.

JONES: How do you know when your students are developing a spiritual understanding of technique? Do you see it? Do you feel it?

SAOTOME SENSEI: First, I know how to kill other people. But what is harder is to know how to help other people survive. Very difficult. How to heal other people. Easy to crush other people, but how can you heal other people?

JONES: How does someone learn to do that?

SAOTOME SENSEI: Same power, but different aspect—healing and crushing. Same power but mental difference.

JONES: How do I learn to heal others?

SAOTOME SENSEI: This is *satori!* A message from God.

JONES: Should all martial art technique be about healing other people?

SAOTOME SENSEI: It depends on your mind. Some can know this and some cannot—yet. Do you wish to crush or heal? Make a choice, but that is only the beginning. It is in your character. If you carry hatred, you destroy other people and destroy yourself. The education of budo is about refining your . . . changing hatred to healing. Anger is important. Hatred is important.

JONES: How is it important?

SAOTOME SENSEI: How do you define the difference? You have hatreds, Jones?

JONES: I . . . .

SAOTOME SENSEI: You can tell me that you don't have hatreds?

JONES: Yes, I have hatreds.

SAOTOME SENSEI: Of course, because you have great love. You hate people who are arrogant? You hate people who hurt other people? You hate them.

JONES: I don't like such people . . . .

SAOTOME SENSEI: Because?

JONES: I . . . .

SAOTOME SENSEI: Think about freedom and limitations. Think about great love and great hatred. You don't think so?

JONES: I understand what you are saying, but I would like to think that . . . .

SAOTOME SENSEI: You would like to think that you are free too.

JONES: What about Hitler? He had great hatred, but you are saying that he also had great love?

SAOTOME SENSEI: It is not about right and wrong. Hitler had great love. In his mind he loved his country, loved his family, loved his position in power. Narrow love. But, of course. It is naive to think that great love and great hate exist independent from each other. It makes your thinking confused. You can hate for moral reasons and love for immoral reasons. It is about balance. It is like a shadow. I deeply respect Jesus Christ, but his book, the Bible, is responsible for many innocent people being killed. True?

JONES: I would have to agree with that.

SAOTOME SENSEI: I try to see reality.

JONES: On another subject, have you noticed any change in Western martial arts students over the past ten or twenty years?

SAOTOME SENSEI: They think about it more nowadays. Better educated to it then twenty years ago. It makes my job both harder and easier. People see more possibilities in martial arts today than twenty years ago. Then it was very much about fighting. I see more and more Western students coming to understanding that martial arts are not about fighting. People's concepts are becoming broader. This is the result of education.

JONES: Do you think that martial arts are better off today than twenty years ago?

SAOTOME SENSEI: Yes. People today are looking for more. They expect more. There is more. I agree with that. But—one thing, philosophy is just confusing. Budo is not philosophy. It is universal truth. People make philosophy in their brains. Universe does not make philosophy—just reality. Philosophy is what separates this martial art and that martial art. The reality they must deal with are universal. Deal with universal reality.

JONES: Thank you very much for your time, sensei.

SAOTOME SENSEI: One more thing. Try to help people and you can never go wrong.

The Karatedoka:
An Interview with Professor Thomas Cauley

Professor Thomas Cauley is a stellar example of a Westerner who has been deeply enriched by his practice of the martial arts of Japan. On October 3, 1999, he was promoted to eighth-degree black belt by Masanao Yamazaki, Roshi and Director of Sakugawa Koshiki Shorinji-ryu karatedo. At present he serves as International Director for Ryujin Kempo Jutsu and the All Japan Karatedo Kempo Federation, centered in Kogawara-mura, Japan. He also heads the Isshinkaikan Institute of Karatedo and Kempo, which comprises forty-five dojos and 108 black belts.

Cauley began his study of Shorinji-ryu in 1957, in Virginia Beach, Virginia, under the instruction of Asaki Masayuki Sensei. He enlisted in the Air Force in 1961 and was stationed at Fuchu Air Station, Japan. Seeking further instruction in karatedo, he joined the dojo of Ueki Masaaki Sensei. In 1963 he began to study also with Okada Jiro, a fifth-degree black belt in Sakugawa Koshiki Shorinji-ryu karatedo and Yuishinkai kobudo systems.

In 1966 Cauley was posted to Thailand, where he received a medal from the king of Thailand for his efforts in teaching karatedo. Upon transfer to Misawa Air Base, Japan, he met Ogasawara Tokushiro, headmaster of Sakugawa Koshiki Shorinji-ryu. The bulk of Cauley's karatedo training occurred under Ogasawara Shihan, who promoted him to seventh-degree black belt in 1976. Ogasawara Shihan died in 1986. The current headmaster of Sakugawa Koshiki Shorinji-ryu is Ogasawara (Ando) Teikeishiro. His successor will be ninth-degree black belt Narita Satoru Shihan.

Professor Cauley was also greatly influenced by his participation in the practices of the Kongokyo Zen sect under the guidance of Yamazaki Masanao Roshi, who died recently of congestive heart failure.

JONES: How would you suggest that a Westerner prepare for the opportunity to practice budo in Japan?

CAULEY: Mental and physical preparation is necessary. Books on budo, history, and the classics are always good. It also pays to be in top physical condition before attempting even the rudiments of budo.

JONES: What are some of the worst mistakes a Westerner can make while practicing budo in Japan?

CAULEY: Boasting, bragging. Lack of sincerity. Not paying attention to basic etiquette and the seriousness of budo.

JONES: If a Western student had only three things to keep in mind to make his or her budo training in Japan most personally profitable, what would those three things be?

CAULEY: Humbleness, sincerity, and a quiet demeanor.

JONES: What are some of the differences and similarities between budo practice in the United States and budo practice in Japan?

CAULEY: For the most part Westerners know a great deal of technique, history, and armchair philosophy. Eastern students may know less, but what they do know they know much better. In the West karatedo is usually taught in one of four ways: many practice it as a sport, some as an art, some for self-defense, and some enjoy the science of it. For the art aspect, it must be steeped in esotericism. For the self-defense aspect, *it must work.* From the point of view of science, it must be related to natural principles, including geomancy and mathematics.

The most important thing to understand is that, in Japan, karatedo—as all arts—is practiced for self-perfection. I spent six years at

Rokunoheji [a Zen monastery] in Aomori Prefecture. One of the things I learned was to seek the Zen in karatedo. Zen in karatedo gives us an immediate view of Zen in its active phase. Master Yamazaki of Rokunoheji taught me that karatedo is active Zen, while contemplation is passive Zen. Karatedo becomes Zen-oriented immediately in that it is an expression of nature and naturalness at its highest levels. The very techniques of karatedo involve the "art of artlessness," what Master Ogasawara Tokushiro called the "controlled accident," like a leaf falling.

JONES: What is the first thought that comes to you when I ask, what did Zen teach you?

Cauley: Hurry, and all things it involves, is fatal. Patience is crucial to us as students of karatedo, especially with regard to rank, learning numbers of *kata*, gaining technical skills, and so on. The karatedo sensei watches a student the way a gardener watches a tree grow. You might think of a tree: it grows purposelessly, there are no short-cuts to being a tree, every step is both the beginning and the end. This attitude can best be nurtured through daily contemplation and meditation. Yes, patience, and also tolerance, are so important because they are the basis of peace. We must hold that everyone is entitled to his or her opinion or philosophy, just as we have our own. We cannot say that we alone have the truth. Education, instruction, and enlightenment are the tools with which we can fight intolerance and fanaticism. Karatedo is not a religion, nor is Zen. This must be understood immediately. Anybody who would make karatedo or Zen a religion falsifies it, denaturalizes it. Karatedo is life. Life is karatedo. There is no pretense in karatedo.

JONES: If you had a few minutes to speak to one of your students before they boarded an airplane for Japan for budo training, what would you tell them?

CAULEY: Continuity is the magic word in the art. Keep right on blocking, punching, and kicking. On and on and on. You must have patience and feel your way from stone to stone because you have never walked this path before. Be cautious and patient. The path of enlightenment ascends upwards, and ever upwards. You must make yourself your friend. The dojo must remain as a holy place because enlightenment is represented in it. It is a place where ignorance, greed, animosity, violence, and prejudice should be set aside.

JONES: What are the roles of nature and natural movements?

CAULEY: You must become one with nature, with the universal. Familiarity with nature increases our love for truth and freedom. The purpose of karatedo is to make people wise. Mere knowledge is not sufficient. Do not lose the true sight of the reason you study karatedo: to add to your state of wisdom. Being able to duplicate all the movements and receive all the philosophy does not make you a wise person. It is simply borrowed knowledge. Mere knowledge brings no one closer to the truth; mere knowledge makes no one more free—and in some cases fits one better for servitude or slavery. You have to be beyond technique, beyond knowledge.

Ishi kowasu! [Smash the stone!]

The Four Philosophical Worlds of Budo

Westerners commonly associate Japanese martial arts and Zen Buddhism. While I would say that all Japanese martial arts are about Zen (in the sense of a mental/spiritual practice of refinement), they are not all about Zen Buddhism. While Buddhism does exert its influence, so do Shintoism and Confucianism, and, of course, bushido, the code of the warrior.

When you enter a Japanese dojo, you will see visual representations of all four worlds. The ranking and organization of the dojo will be based on Confucian ideals, while the shrine in front of the dojo may feature a Zen Buddhist–inspired work of calligraphy or flower arrangement. On the wall, high above the dojo floor, one will often see a *kamidana*, or Shinto shrine. The interactions of the members of the dojo will be prescribed by Confucian rules of conduct and ranking and by bushido, a code heavily indebted to Confucian thought.

The interesting point is that these ideas are so deeply entrenched in Japanese culture that the Japanese *budoka* may not be overtly aware of them, although they are being guided by their notions of correct procedure and thought. The Japanese find no problem in grouping "religious" ideas and reacting to them in terms of context. One Japanese colleague once said, only half jokingly, "We Japanese do business like Christians, marry like Shintoists, and are buried as Buddhists." In a similar vein, when I was doing my research before going to Japan, I read several studies showing that when the Japanese population was polled concerning religious beliefs, the combined numbers of people who claimed to be Buddhist or Shintoist or Christian far exceeded the total population of Japan! In other words, the Japanese were acknowledging that they could be Buddhist and Shintoist at the same time, depending on the context.

Each of the four philosophical worlds of budo offers specific ideas about the nature and goal of budo practice. Professor Inazo Nitobe, author of *Bushido: The Warrior's Code*, discusses this subject in the chapter "Sources of Bushido." (pp. 17-21). He writes of Buddhism, for example: "Buddhism had three basic tenets: Sense of calm; trust in fate; submission to the inevitable, disdain for life coupled with friendliness with death, and a stoic composure in the face of calamity. These are all embodied in the code of bushido."

Of Zen Buddhism he notes (p. 17), "The method of Zen is contemplation and the achievement of excellence. One of the highest attainments of a master of any of the military arts was to also become a Zen master." I would add that the terms *mushin* (empty mind) and *zanshin* (remaining mind) both found throughout Japanese martial arts, derive from Buddhism, in which mind is much more of a central concept than in Shinto, Confucianism, or bushido.

Shinto ("the way of the gods") is a very parochial religion, though based on sources more ancient than Buddhism, Confucianism, or bushido. Whereas Buddhism, Confucianism, and *bushido* can be directly transmitted to the West, Shinto remains tied to the physical environment of Japan, "home of the gods." Places where *kami* (spirits or gods) were believed to dwell became important Shinto shrine sites. It is a religion that unites the Japanese people with their physical environment and their history. Shinto is about loyalty to the land, rulers of the land, and one's family, both living and dead; it is about purity, devotion, the physical aspects of living, community identity, celebration of existence, and a belief in what Nitobe calls (p. 17) "the God-like purity of the human soul." Hence it led to the "infallibility of conscience."

Shinto also has a mystical side, which Nitobe did not address: a belief that mere mortals can interact directly with spiritual forces. Today a visitor to Japan can, for example, see *miko* (priestesses) at Shinto sites, sweeping the grounds or acting as cashiers in booths that sell shrine charms of various kinds. They are usually identified by their red hakama and white kimono. Originally, they were spirit mediums who would channel the voices of the *kami* of the shrine to the waiting faithful.

Another important concept of mystical Shinto is *kannagara no michi*, which means something like "the flowing path of God's love." This phrase suggests that the unifying sacred threads interwoven throughout all realms of existence can be experienced by mere mortals and that in so doing one can literally become what one identifies with, in this case "divine energy."

The founders of Japanese martial arts schools often have had religious experiences in which they believe a communication has occurred between them and *kami* (Shinto spirits/gods). The *tengu* (long-nosed forest goblins), Shinto *kami* of the local type, were said to be especially important in imparting important skills to the sincere martial artist.

Nitobe (p. 17) refers to Confucius as "one of the most prolific sources of bushido." Confucius's "Five Moral Relationships" were the foundation of bushido. These relationships—master to servant, father to son, husband to wife, older to younger siblings, and friend to friend—were believed by Confucius and his followers to be a kind of natural law, the "way of heaven." Confucius argued that knowledge must be shown through action or it was empty. He taught that everything one does must be guided by correct behavioral principles. Interacting with an emperor, knowing how to dress correctly on a spring day, understanding proper deportment at a funeral, all came under the scrutiny of Confucius. He taught that proper formal behavior was a means to cement a community with a familial sense. This aspect of Confucianism is the reason that members of a dojo relate to each other in familial ways. The sensei is your father/mother. His/her peers are your uncles. Students are your elder brothers and younger brothers, elder sisters and younger sisters.

Bushido is rudimentarily about relationships among warriors and their leaders, but these relationships are all informed by Shinto, Buddhist, and Confucian about duty, relationship, loyalty, and obligation. The various -isms discussed above all blend in the Japanese warriors' code of behavior.

Just as every dojo you enter will show evidence of influence from Shintoism, Buddhism, Confucianism, and bushido, each will also, regardless of style being practiced, utilize a set of fundamental terms. Such concepts, in that they are universal in Japanese budo, suggest that they must be extremely ancient.

First, the word *katsu!* I begin with this exclamation (pronounced *khats!*) to point out that the martial arts terms may be as much about a feeling as about direct reference to some object, philosophical notion, method of attack, or part of the body. *Osu!* and *yoshi!* are other examples.

I first encountered *katsu* while studying Zen literature. In an exchange between master and monk, the following was not uncommon: "Student: Master, what is Buddha nature? Master: *Katsu!*"

It is a shout with no rational content. It is *kiai*. My first experience with *katsu* was in kyudo practice. I managed in a matter of months to adequately learn the basic shooting form, but my *sempai* indicated something was still missing. She finally resorted to *katsu* out of frustration with me, it seemed. As I prepared to shoot one morning under the watchful eye of Asakuma Sensei's second in command, I could see deep frown lines in her forehead as she watched me and mumbled to herself in Japanese. Finally, she stepped close to me, and her eyebrows shot up, her eyes widened, and she shouted what sounded to me like "guts!" Then it struck me. I had just heard a real *katsu!* At the most basic level, it means something like "Put some spirit into it!" or "Get fired up!" The *sempai*, because she could not speak English and I could not speak Japanese, was, through a word, trying to reach and ignite the place of my spirit.

Katsu relates to one of the most important universal concepts in the Japanese martial arts, *hara*. When my *sempai* "uttered the *katsu*" as they say in the Zen literature, it clearly came from her *hara*, her belly or lower abdomen. The *hara* might be visualized as existing about two inches below the navel and in the center of the abdominal area. Sometimes the location of this important site is diced more finely. In the writings of the Tokugawa-period Zen master Hakuin Zenji, called "the reviver of Rinzai Zen" and the main focus of all the inspirational talks of the *roshi* of Shofukuji in Fukuoka, one finds that Master Hakuin differentiated between the *kikai*, which he referred to as the center of breathing, and which is located about an inch and a half below the navel, and the *tanden*, which he called the center of strength and which is found two inches below the navel (Yampolsky, 1971:30).

All martial arts will constantly exhort you to focus on the *hara*, to move from the *hara*, to punch from the *hara*, to breath from the *hara*. The *hara*, the center, the *tan t'ien* (Chinese), is not only the center of your physical body, but also the center of your mental and spiritual self.

To a Westerner, the emphasis on the *hara* is sometimes mockingly referred to as "meditating on your belly-button." But I think the West understands the *hara*. The football coach used to exhort us to have a "gut check" as a way of encouraging us when we were down. In other words, the "gut" (*hara*) was used by the coach and easily understood by the players to mean exactly what *hara* means: a physical, mental, and spiritual center in the lower abdomen—a place where somehow you can find strength and inspiration. The football coach also instructed us to tackle the ball carrier's "belt buckle," yet another way of indicating the *hara*.

When traveling in Wyoming some years back I stopped at a small local rodeo. There were no seats and all the participants were friends and neighbors. To stand next to the corral listening to the cowboys comment on the events, joke with each other, and tell stories was every American boy's dream when I was growing up. As I enjoyed the family-style rodeo I heard a man's voice boom out, "Ride him in your belly, Danny! Ride him in your belly!" In the corral a cowboy was trying to stay astride a bucking horse as his friend advised him to use the principle of *hara*.

In Japan deep and intimate communication between two individuals is thought of as being generated by the *hara*. The term "belly arts" (*haragei*) indicates skill at interpersonal communication. The martial arts are about communication. The best martial art is encapsulated in a kind of behavior that communicates to a would-be attacker that you are unassailable. If you know the truth of that statement from the *hara*, you are likely to be unassailable.

The *hara* can be physically experienced. The first time I experienced my *hara* was in meditation with Chan Poi Sifu. The kung fu teacher had earlier in the week instructed us in a type of breathing meditation which focused mental attention on the *tan t'ien*, the area called *hara* in Japanese. About an hour into meditation one day I felt something moving in my abdomen. It felt like something alive was wriggling around in my belly. As I tried to visualize what I was feeling, I received the mental image of a ball a little bigger than a golf ball composed of tiny lizards or little snakes. The tingling or wriggling sensation in a small area in my abdomen enabled me to focus my attention on my *hara* with more intensity, and the more I focused, the more the little ball of lizards wiggled. I later read about the Kundalini experience in Hindu belief in which the yogi feels a snake in the pit of his stomach which slowly rises up the spine and creates, they say, all sorts of wondrous spiritual experiences. My experience did have the wriggling quality of the Kundalini serpent, but it is envisioned as a divine cobra in yoga whereas all I had was a ball of stunted lizards. More practice is probably called for.

Hara, in the meaning of "body center," might also be understood in terms of horsemanship. Most of the Chinese martial arts refer to their stances as "horses." A major series of *kata* in Japanese karatedo is called Ironclad Horsemen, and we've already seen the American cowboy's contribution to the art of the center. If you can image yourself as a mounted knight as you perform your art's techniques, you will move toward a centered and *hara*-conscious method of martial art. The horse (you from the waist down) rises and falls and steps over obstacles, while the rider (you from the waist up), his/her seat firmly attached to the saddle (the middle), maintains an elegant body alignment, allowing the horse to do all the heavy lifting.

A physical demonstration of *hara* is produced whenever one generates a "belly laugh." Nervous, tense individuals tend to express laughter as giggling, or high-pitched shrieks. Those who are acting from the *hara* produce the belly laugh. My kyudo Sensei, Asakuma Shihan, laughed like Mae West, with a deep and almost bawdy rumble. Her laughter came from her center and it spoke of relaxation, energy, and joy. My *shakuhachi* sensei (flute teacher) at Saikoji, where I practiced Komuso Zen, had a laugh that made me think of Santa Claus.

The *hara* for the Japanese serves many of the same symbolic functions as the Western notion of the heart. When we want to express deep emotion we touch our heart. We express loyalty to our country by placing our hand over our heart. We express great love to another by touching our heart. We express sincerity by touching our heart. But like the *hara*, if you tried to find the place in the actual heart organ where love or deep sincerity dwells, you would be no more likely to find it than a Japanese surgeon operating to locate the *hara*. But, like the Japanese, our culture makes us feel "right" when we attach to the heart all sorts of non-material, symbolic, and emotional intent.

The mention of attachment leads to the next important universal martial arts conception, that of *musubi* (sticking; also harmonious interaction, and unity of purpose). Everything in the martial arts is about *musubu*. In *kumite* (free fighting), you must *musubu*. When throwing in aikido, you must *musubu*. You also must "harmoniously interact" with your bow and arrows in Kyudo, your sword in iaido practice, and the *jo* and *bokken* of jodo. *Musubi* does not suggest dependence such as, "He is attached to his mother," but rather a kind mutuality of purpose. The best *musubi* I have experienced lately came from a bumblebee I encountered one afternoon in my garden. When I became aware that the bee was going to light on my hand, I moved it. The bee, however, seemed to be attached to an area about one to three inches from my skin. No matter how I waved my hands and arms, the bee stuck to me, without actually touching me. It just seemed to become part of me in some way. Wherever I went, it was there. Martial arts teachers come in all shapes and sizes—and species.

Ki is *the* big concept in the Japanese martial arts. You find this component in many Japanese words: *tenki* (weather; "heaven's *ki*"), *kuki* (air; *ki* of the sky, or void), *tanki* (impatient; "short *ki*"), *byoki* (illness; sick *ki*), *kichigai* (crazy; distorted *ki*), and so forth.

Ki indicates the energy that is the driving force of the universe. Its origin is divine. It exists in all things, including humans, and can be exercised and strengthened. You can lose it; you can gain it. Everything works better with it and seems to fall apart without it. It is what my kyudo *sempai* was trying to ignite with her *katsu!* It is what enables the adept to break rocks with their bare hands. It is an energy that never dies but only transmutes. The *hara* is the major charging center for *ki* in the body. "The fire in the belly" we call it.

For a Westerner the concept may lead to a new way of understanding the unity of all things, by borrowing and internalizing a Japanese concept. Or we may understand that this concept is not all that mystical from a Westerner's viewpoint. If you tell martial arts students to put more "spirit" or "enthusiasm" into their *kata* or practice of basic technique, you are directly addressing their conscious ability to augment their *ki,* or energy, by an act of will. This is a beginning. Once the martial artist realizes that the energy put into the act is the energy received back from the act, *ki* becomes an everyday companion. It is "is-ness," but it moves. It advances. It retreats. It gets sick. It becomes misled. It can be stored. It is your enthusiasm. It is your oomph! Once you are on friendly terms with *ki,* you are ready for the next big leap.

Which brings us to Zen, or meditation. All Japanese martial arts will utilize Zen. Remember that Zen and Zen Buddhism are not necessarily the same thing. You will recognize others in a Zen state of practice by their self-containment, their ignoring of distraction, their intensity of being, their inwardness, their focus. You can see it in their eyes and in the quiet but dense energy that seems to emanate from them. Everything one does in a dojo should be Zen. My karatedo sensei referred to *kata* performance as "showing your Zen." The intense mental focus of the jodo sensei, expressed through their eyes, their *kamai* (facing attitude), and their *kiai,* was just about unbearable to stand against as they approached you across the floor with sword raised, their eyes staring unblinkingly into yours. The blocking and parrying with the *jo* against the *bokken* was nothing compared to maintaining and returning the focused gaze of an attacking jodo *shihan*.

Master Asakuma's daily firing of two arrows was a virtuoso act of archery, but more than that it was an opportunity to stare Zen in the face. When she shot, one could feel her intensity of focus, her aloneness, and the bond (*musubi*) between Asakuma Sensei, her bow and arrows, and the target. Nothing else existed for her at that moment. She was in deep Zen.

The formal methods of meditation taught by the various *ryu* can be based on various types of breathing, exercises which coordinate breathing and body movement, the shooting of an arrow, the drawing of a sword, or the performance of *kata*. They are meant to introduce the student to meditation as well as to a technique passed down through the history of the *ryu*. One art I practiced used bells in meditation. The Komuso Zen monks used large bamboo flutes. I practiced in dojo that used drums, gongs, hollow wooden fish, and sticks struck sharply together. It is all fundamentally the same act. However, the joining with the meditation style of your dojo will energize your Zen, as well as enhance your rapport with dojo mates. The end point is to be Zen, not to be forever practicing Zen, or some would say that to be forever practicing Zen is to be Zen. They also talk about one hand clapping, and the look on your face before you were born. Accept the puzzle of it all—the four worlds—and enjoy allowing these ancient notions to instruct you. Try to clearly perceive the contributions of Buddhism, Confucianism, Shintoism, and bushido to the mind-set of Japanese warriors, but don't try too hard. Go at it as if you were taking a walk in a heavy fog. Go slowly and you will get thoroughly wet.

Some Parting Comments

Don't be overwhelmed by the information you have just read. The rules of practice in a particular dojo; the teachings embodied in the dojokun; the detailed nature of the simple bow; the often mystical, mythological, and quasi-historical notions underlying the various martial arts; concepts such as *hara* and *ki* and *mushin*; awareness of the typically complex and acrimonious divisions of the various ryu; and the complexity of the various *kata* and *kihon waza* of the style you choose to practice are, taken together, an awesome burden. This is as it should be. Learning to bear up under pressure, to gladly take on burdens that make us stronger, are at the very marrow of the way of the warrior.

It is helpful to understand that even many Japanese don't understand the nature of correct budo behavior. My karatedo sensei in America once told us that we would possibly come to learn more about budo history and culture than the average Japanese. At the time I thought that was a rather extreme statement, but my experience in Japan demonstrated that he was accurate in his comment.

As a university professor teaching in Japan I was assigned a Japanese colleague, my "closest colleague," at each of the educational institutions at which I taught. These men and women were to help me deal with the Japanese educational institutions—translations during lectures, the typical paperwork of a university professor, grading student papers—as well as the myriad details of simply living in a foreign country. Once while walking in a local park with one of them I heard the sound of archery. This was to lead to my first contact with Asakuma Shihan and the Fukuoka Budokan *kyudojo*. I asked my friend if he would speak with the sensei about the possibility of my joining the archery group. Although I could clearly see that this suggestion caused him some anxiety he nevertheless approached Asakuma Shihan and made the request. Afterwards, he commented to me, "That's the first time I ever talked with a budo sensei." On a similar occasion I asked another colleague to arrange for me to interview a Shinto priest. The interview was arranged but again came the comment, "I never talked to a Shinto priest before."

I was invited to speak before a college group in the town of Kumamoto, located in the center of the island of Kyushu. I knew from my reading in the martial arts that this was the place the great Musashi spent his last days. When asked what I would require for an honorarium, or speaker's fee, I told them that I would like to be taken to Regando cave, the place where Musashi wrote *Gorin no Sho*, to his burial site, and to the museum where his swords, *bokken*, and paintings were displayed.

These visits were arranged, but I soon found that I was the only one in the group of Japanese English teachers and college professors who even knew who Musashi was! It was surreal to stand on his burial mound outside of Kumamoto and recount to the teachers a story that seemed to me so integral in the mythology of Japanese warrior heroes. As I spoke to the group, I noted that I had observed that one of the subway stops in Kumamoto was Musashi Tsuka, or "the burial mound of Musashi." I was told that the group knew the subway stop but did not know what it meant or to what historical figure it pointed.

One of the most shocking instances of observing the Japanese citizen behaving in total ignorance of what even a Western student of Japanese culture would know came during my time at Shofukuji, the Zen temple. It is customary in all circumstances, not just at Zen temples, to wear a special pair of "toilet shoes" into a restroom. These shoes are generally located at the entrance to the toilet. The custom is to slip out of the rice-straw sandals we were required to wear else-where at the temple, to slip into the rubber "toilet shoes" to enter the toilet, and then to slip out of the specially provided shoes and back into our sandals before entering the *zendo* (meditation hall). This is absolutely rudimentary behavior in Japan. It is a very fundamental act of cleanliness and respect.

One evening, however, as we sat in meditation, a middle-aged woman arrived late for Zen practice. As she entered the *zendo*, some-thing sounded wrong. Instead of the quite "shush, shush" sound that one makes when walking in rice-straw sandals, this woman's steps sounded like "plip-plop, plip-plop." It was the sound of rubber san-dals—toilet shoes! Seated on the raised platforms that lined the *zendo*, I could see the woman's shoes as she walked past me. My sus-picions were confirmed. I couldn't believe what I was seeing. At about that moment, I heard the senior monk explode into action. Out of the corner of my eye. I saw him hurtle off the meditation platform, grab the *kyosaku*, and charge the poor woman with a shattering *kiai*. The offender quickly backpedaled from the enraged monk's advance. As she reached the doorsill, she tripped and tumbled into a low hedge that surrounded the zendo. Satisfied with that, the senior monk har-rumphed, turned and quietly returned to his sitting place. I never saw the woman again.

You are not Japanese, so don't try to be. Study of Japanese cultural manners is an art in itself. In its complexity it is beyond the grasp of a short-time visitor to Japan except in its most basic form. Count on the fact that your sincerity of practice will excuse lapses in eti-quette that you are not trained to be aware of, also remembering that even the Japanese make procedural errors and fundamental mistakes in politeness.

Sometimes Westerners will attempt to "become" Japanese as they practice a martial art in Japan. This can be seen in the broken "Japlish" (English-Japanese pronunciation) they begin to affect. The very essence of budo is about becoming your true self, not some walking caricature of a Westerner trying to act like Toshiro Mifune in a samurai movie.

The martial arts of Japan cannot be understood apart from the cultural context in which they are found. In the West, martial artists find much complex meaning in what they believe are the arcane and mysterious behaviors of the traditional dojo. However, to a great extent, the behavior in a Japanese dojo is simply a reaffirmation of basic Japanese everyday behavior—bowing, hierarchical awareness of rank, emphasis on group harmony, mutual support among group members, belief in the wisdom of the body, honoring of ancient ideas about students and teachers, respecting neighbors, community, and nation, and honoring the ancient samurai roots of Japanese high culture. Therefore, don't think of the Japanese martial arts as somehow separate from everyday life. To be a good budoka one must understand the society in which one finds himself or herself. This is a fundamental martial principle, by the way. How would one know what to do martially without understanding the contextual sociocultural situation?

In order to touch the *shizen* (naturalness) aspects of budo one must gain some control over everyday life in Japan. The same rules that are used in the dojo will be found as neighbor relates to neighbor and community to community. Once you gain some insight into "normal" life in Japan your actions in the dojo will seem more sincere and integrated, at least from the perspective of your sensei, and that is the only perspective worth cultivating.

Mundane though it may be, you should give consideration to the practice uniform and weapons you may require while training in Japan. My height made all of the Japanese weapons too short. In jodo, the short staffs provided by the budokan club for student practice were about six inches too short. I literally could not execute a wide range of jodo techniques because of the relatively short size of the typical *jo*. I finally had to cut a karatedo *bo* (six-foot staff) to fit my height. I had similar problems trying to fit *tonfa* and *sai* to my body size. This problem also holds for *dogi* and *hakama*. The Japanese martial arts supply stores are not accustomed to customers who stand over six feet tall. If you are in this height range, buy your practice uniform and weapons in the United States and take them to Japan, or you will be cursed to bear the mark of the foreign martial arts student—*hakama* that come to mid-calf and *dogi* sleeves that don't reach much past your elbows. The problem of obtaining practice clothing can be ameliorated, however, by tailors who will custom-make your outfits. They are not hard to find although they will be expensive. A *dogi* that fits well or a *hakama* that hangs right does make a difference in your practice. I took my *dogi* and *hakama* with me when I went to Japan. Still, I had to purchase a custom-made *dogi* top for Kyudo practice since my *judogi* was not practical for shooting a bow and arrow.

Tall Westerners seem to constantly amaze many Japanese. When I was taken to a specialized tailor shop to be outfitted as a Rinzai Zen monk (Komuso monks being affiliated with this major branch of Zen Buddhism), all of the seamstresses emerged from the back rooms of the establishment to marvel at how much material it would take to make my kimono.

The costume is important for the overall look of the art. It is distracting to watch a martial arts practitioner with clothing and equipment that doesn't fit. Dignity and symmetry are lost, or at least seriously dented.

As far as preparing for your trip to Japan, understand that you have been preparing for that moment your whole life. You are not going to suddenly change once you are in Japan. You will be the person you have unconsciously or consciously practiced to be your whole life. If I could suggest some avenues of preparation that are possible, I would point to readings on Japanese contemporary culture, history, and budo behavior; stretching; endurance and stamina training; meditation; and interviews with others who have practiced martial arts in Japan.

Education was always noted by the samurai to be of great importance. "The sword and the pen are one" was a typical saying. You won't know what is going on around you without studying, and not to know what is going on around you is to be a warrior who is about to be killed. Budo carries its own internal wisdom. A warrior must have knowledge. A warrior must understand social and cultural conditions. This is a basic, fundamental reality of all warfare.

I emphasize stretching because it is crucial for safely practicing a strenuous art or sport and because it connects to an overall relaxation of the body which is key to all martial arts practice. As such it links with meditation, as hatha yoga demonstrates so effectively. There are a million forms of meditation, but they all share one common feature: they are about being precisely in the present moment and not wandering mentally in the past or future. You may sit and count your breaths for half an hour morning and evening. You may chant to yourself the word "one" for half an hour morning and evening. You may punch a *makiwara* five hundred times a day and achieve a similar effect. Or you may watch a rock grow. At the very highest level, one simply "watches" his or her mind. The importance of meditation and martial arts is historically witnessed by the fact that Zen Buddhism made its first heavy impact on Japanese culture when it was embraced by the warrior class during the Kamakura period, the era when Rinzai Zen and Soto Zen were promulgated throughout Japan.

Don't expect that all Japanese will automatically understand and applaud your decision to go to Japan for budo training. Some will. Some will not. You may find that many young Japanese find the whole idea of budo unpalatable due to its association with conservative and old-fashioned values. The Japanese college students I taught at Seinan Gakuin and Kyushu University were split on the issue. One group saw budo more as a sport than some type of spiritual path, while others rejected entirely the right-wing political implications of budo and its feudal structure. They were particularly critical of the excesses often reached in the *sempai-kohai* relationship. I often found myself in the position of arguing for the many benefits of budo training to Japanese college students who were very negative toward the whole idea.

One day I heard the phrase *henna gaijin* being applied to me. When I asked what it meant, my Japanese friend said with obvious embarrassment, "It means 'crazy foreigner.'" I must have registered surprise on my face because he hastily added, "There is a story about an American named Mr. Smith and his old Japanese friend Mr. Saito. Every year they would climb Mt. Fuji together. At the end of one such trek, as they were resting, Mr. Smith said to Mr. Saito, 'What does your family think of you making this hike every year?' Mr. Saito replied, 'They think it brings me great merit.' Mr. Smith continued,

'And what does your family think of me making this hike each year?'
'Oh,' said Mr. Saito, 'they think you are crazy.'"

The bottom line is for you to relax and enjoy your training in Japan. Work through budo to discover who you really are. Be sincere. Be humble. Try as hard as you can, and don't ever stop. *Gambatte!*

Bibliography

Finn, Michael. *Iaido: The Way of the Sword.* London: Paul H. Crompton Ltd., 1982.

Leggett, Trevor. *Zen and the Ways.* Tokyo: Tuttle Publishing, 1978.

Lovret, Frederick J. *The Way and the Power.* Boulder, Colorado: Paladin Press. 1987.

Nitobe, Inazo. Bushido: *The Warrior's Code.* Boston: Tuttle Publishing, 1979.

Random, Michel. *The Martial Arts.* London: Peerage Books, 1984.

Ueshiba, Morihei (trans. John Stevens). *Budo.* New York: Kodansha International, 1991.

Williams, Bryn (ed.). *Martial Arts of the Orient.* London: Hamlyn, 1975.

Wilson, William S. *The Ideals of The Samurai: Writings of Japanese Warriors.* Burbank, California: Ohara Publications, Inc., 1982.

Yampolsky, Philip B. (ed.). *Zen Master Hakuin: Selected Writings.* New York: Columbia University Press, 1971.

Web Sites Listed in the Text

www.gojuryu.net
—Goju-ryu Karatedo

www.iskf.com
—International Shotokan Karate Federation (Philadelphia)

plaza27.mbn.or.jp/~kkaname/skif/skif_e.htm
—Shotokan Karatedo International Federation

www.kyokushin.co.jp
—International Karate Organization Kyokushinkaikan

www.shorinjikempo.or.jp
—Shorinji Kempo

www.kendo-usa.org
—All United States Kendo Federation

www.aikikai.org
—Aikikai Hombu Dojo (Aikikai World Headquarters)

www.aikiweb.com
—AikiWeb: The Source for Aikido Information

www.daito-ryu.org
—Daito-ryu Aiki Jujutsu Home Page

www.ninjutsu.com
—American Bujinkan Dojo